158.1

Items should be returned on or before the date shown below. Items
not already requested by other borrowers may be renewed in person,
in writing or by telephone. To renew, please quote the number on the
barcode label. To renew online a PIN is required. This can be requested
at your local library.
Renew online @ **www.dublincitypubliclibraries.ie**
Fines charged for overdue items will include postage incurred in recovery.
Damage to or loss of items will be charged to the borrower.

Leabharlanna Poiblí Chathair Bhaile Átha Cliath
Dublin City Public Libraries

Raheny Branch
Tel: 8315521

Comhairle Cathrach
Bhaile Átha Cliath
Dublin City Council

Due Date	Due Date	Due Date

dept.store *for* the mind

AS

YOU

ARE

A GUIDE TO LETTING GO OF COMPARISON AND SEEING THE GOOD STUFF INSIDE

aster

An Hachette UK Company

www.hachette.co.uk

First published in Great Britain in 2018 by Aster, an imprint of Octopus Publishing Group Ltd

Carmelite House

50 Victoria Embankment

London EC4Y 0DZ

www.octopusbooks.co.uk

Distributed in the US by Hachette Book Group

1290 Avenue of the Americas

4th and 5th Floors

New York, NY 10104

Distributed in Canada by Canadian Manda Group

664 Annette St.

Toronto, Ontario, Canada

M6S 2C8

ISBN 978-1-91202-367-7

A CIP catalogue record for this book is available from the British Library.

Printed and bound in China

10 9 8 7 6 5 4 3 2 1

Consultant Publisher Kate Adams

Consultant Editor Ruth Williams

Junior Editor Ella Parsons

Copy Editor Nikki Sims

Senior Designer Jaz Bahra at Octopus

Creative Direction and Design Katie Steel, Jo Raynsford and Nicky Collings at Supafrank

Illustrator Karolin Schnoor

Pattern Illustration Katie Steel and Chloe Robertson

Production Manager Caroline Alberti

Disclaimer/Publisher's note

All reasonable care has been taken in the preparation of this book but the information it contains is not intended to take the place of treatment by a qualified medical practitioner.

dept.store *for* the mind

BEAUTIFUL WORDS FOR THE MIND

Each book offers stories and ideas about creating daily habits that are kind
to the mind, whether through our connection with nature, our creativity or
everyday tasks, or simply knowing and feeling more accepting of ourselves.
The books stretch the mind and soul, so that we may colour outside the
lines, experience the moments of wonder that are right there in front
of us and occasionally venture out of our safe harbours.

Department Store for the Mind is an exciting new creative venture
offering a place to explore the world inside your head: a vast and
unique terrain of thoughts, ideas, emotions and memories.

www.deptstoreforthemind.com

P.9 | INTRODUCTION

1 | P.10

START
HERE AS
YOU ARE

2 | P.24

COMPARISON
IS THE THIEF
OF JOY

3 | P.38

IT'S NOT PINK
AND IT WAS
NEVER FLUFFY

4 | P.52

STRONG
STUFF

5 | P.68

PERSONAL PUFF

6 | P.82

STRETCH

7 | P.96

TRUST YOUR GUT

8 | P.110

MY WAY

9 | P.124

LAUGHTER
LINES

10 | P.138

THINKING
TRICKS

P.152 | REFERENCES, RESOURCES

AND CREDITS

INTRODUCTION

Swirling beneath the feet of all we do is the vulnerable foundation of our self-belief. The simple act of liking ourselves is the mortar binding the bricks that build our resilience and capacity to cope with whatever life throws at us.

More than that, we want to live a life that's more than functional. We want a life where a steady calm rests within us, and we can enjoy and, indeed, ride the tidal ebb and flow of emotions that are the essence of the human condition.

There is a wealth of research, practice and thinking that can help us to achieve self-acceptance. Some is easy to discover and understand, while some is buried within more complicated language. This book aims to make this wisdom easy to see, easy to understand and, most importantly, easy to put into action.

Within these pages you will find stories from thinkers, writers, psychologists and documentary makers who know what it is to begin to understand and accept yourself as you are. They are all still travelling on their personal journeys and share a chapter of a yet-to-be-completed story.

In a world where so much of the noise around us suggests we are not good enough as we are and that we must seek to change, these accounts try to do something different. They aim to invite a stroll into the complex pathways of the mind to discover the beauty of our own quirky individuality.

As we become more adept at feeling good about our idiosyncrasies, we may become more able to warm to the same funny ways in others. Through tending ourselves, we may go some way to tending our world.

Each chapter offers suggestions and ideas about how to create simple daily habits. Some ideas might work for you, others may pass you by. This is perfectly fine, as there is plenty for each reader to discover a little gem to make their own.

CHAPTER 1

START HERE

AS YOU ARE

START HERE AS YOU ARE

Slowing down to tune in

Ruth Williams | Department Store for the Mind

What if shivers of fear, sinking sensations of dread, the urge to hide away from the world just made you smile?

What if you could roll with it when the average daily ups and downs came and went?

What if something inside your noggin said "It's just part of you, that feeling. Be curious about it. Get to know it. Explore it. Give it colour. Give it sound. Give it smell! Yes, smell... Relish the moment. Hold the moment for as long as you want to. Give it the time it needs."

It's slow living for the mind.

When we slow down we create the space to accept, notice and just let the worry and intensity go.

When we speed up, making ourselves busy and filling every moment with activity, it affects how our brains work. A busy brain with no space to relax and reflect has difficulty seeing the bigger picture.

Most of slow living is good for the mind. This book is an indulgence of the mind first of all. It begins with the mind, rather than the impacts on the mind being the by-product.

Why?

" "

CREATE
SPACE IN
YOUR MIND,
RELEASE
JUDGMENTS
AND EXPLORE
THE WORLD
WITH PLAYFUL
CURIOSITY

Simply, because, when we do something consciously, it sticks in our thinking. Have you ever heard someone say the following about presenting to an audience?

- Tell them what you're going to say or do.

- Say or do it.

- Finish by telling them what you've said and done.

When we start and end with the mind (in mind) we do the same thing. We focus the mind to learn in a certain way. Do the activity. Then reflect to reinforce it, make it stick. And...it works! That's because it reflects how the brain builds its connections: repetition and reinforcement – rewalking our mental pathways – makes them stronger.

Take the idea of beginning a new regime – a morning 15-minute run. Just going out there and running is going to be good for your overall health, reducing stress and giving your body a boost. But to super-charge the benefits for your mind, it's worth making a little time to reflect beforehand on where your mind is, how you are feeling and what background noise is running through your head today. During the run, bring your attention to these observations again and notice any changes. At the end of the run and during the following few hours, check in again on these three things. Over time, as you continue with this practice you will naturally draw attention to the benefits for the mind and, in doing so, begin consciously to enhance their impact.

KINDNESS

This book is all about a way to be kind to yourself. A way to show self-compassion. It's a bit like being a coach for yourself. A great coach won't tell you that you're right or wrong, they will just listen carefully. They will show you that they are listening and ask questions gently and slowly. They'll explore and discover with you. They will look for new angles with you, sometimes just to be curious. They won't push to a solution. Throughout this book we will explore how to do the same thing for yourself.

When Zen Buddhists reach a state of nirvana they are in a place free of judgment. Most of us won't reach that spot quite yet. What we can become aware of is when we make judgments about ourselves and others. Once we've raised this awareness we can start having an inner chat or dialogue with our judgments. As we do this we can find ways to challenge or release them. This book explores all kinds of ways to do this. Some will resonate with you, perhaps, we hope, with earth-moving, toe-tingling, light-bulb-illuminating revelation; others might pass you by or even annoy you slightly. This is fine – there is plenty of advice within these pages. Something for everyone.

> "IT'S JUST PART OF YOU, THAT FEELING.
> BE CURIOUS ABOUT IT. GET TO KNOW IT.
> EXPLORE IT. GIVE IT COLOUR. GIVE IT SOUND.
> GIVE IT SMELL! YES, SMELL…RELISH THE
> MOMENT. HOLD THE MOMENT FOR AS LONG AS
> YOU WANT TO. GIVE IT THE TIME IT NEEDS."

HOW IT STARTED FOR ME

A beautiful, curious little boy came into my life. He made me laugh until my sides really ached; he made me cry with overwhelming bafflement; and he demanded that I revisit the idea of who I was in a way that wasn't too comfortable. Through all this he barely noticed me.

Gyan was autistic, and severely autistic at that. He looked liked any other six-year-old, if the glance was swift. Yet there was far more going on. He showed little interest in forming relationships with anyone, had a strong desire to control and engaged in many repetitious patterns of behaviour. As a first-year undergraduate student, studying Psychology and Drama, I was fascinated.

The Option Institute in the US, led by Barry and Samahria Lyte Kaufman, was working with Gyan and his family, and I signed up to be part of a kind of play-therapy team. We were trained by Gyan's strong, intelligent, inspirational mum, Zenobia. The essence of what we did was to be with Gyan, in a specially designed playroom, and join him in whatever he did. He led and we copied, exactly. Our

job was to immerse ourselves entirely in what he was doing, mirroring every movement, sound, gesture and even eye direction. However, this was just what you saw. The golden heart of this mind-blowing work was about intention – what you were thinking. The intentions we aspired to included:

- I am free to choose my intention (I have a choice about what I think and feel).

- I am totally absorbed by our play together (I let all the background stuff go and, in doing so, gradually become more present in the moment).

- I release judgments as they come and go through my mind.

I struggled with this third one. It wound me up to a point of feeling frustrated and a bit angry. How could you be a human being, going about life day to day, making decisions and keeping safe, without making judgments?

JUDGING JUDGMENTS!

It took some time, perhaps years, but definitely months, for the penny to drop for me about what releasing judgment really meant. Here is how I see the difference:

Judgments:

- Fast food is bad.

- Blonde hair is best.

- My argument is right.

Observations (in this case considered to be free of judgments):

- Fast food gives me tummy ache.

- Blonde hair is popular.

- My argument is based on what I have seen and believe. Yours is based on your own experience. It's probably going to be different because our lives have been different.

This difference between judgment and observation is subtle but crucial. When we observe and notice what happens without jumping to judge, we can see more, it's liberating.

It's liberating because when we judge we decide certain things are right for us and other things are wrong. We then feel the need to act on these judgments in some way and, in doing so, we run the risk of closing our minds to other options or to other people and our connection with them. It seems painfully obvious, but letting go of judgments keeps your options open and the world feeling more interesting and less scary. The beauty in the detail is less likely to pass you by when your mind is open.

Letting go of judging does so much more, though, for your mindset and daily interactions. In my experience, people almost smell judgment on you, with a power equal to that with which they sense acceptance and honest interest. Perhaps it's somehow evident from the words we use and the behaviours we portray. I feel it is something more, maybe something that in time science will be able to measure – after all, evidence for it is everywhere. We could call it intention, as psychologists do, but this word lacks clarity and depth for me. It's belief in part, but it's more than this, too. It's how we feel about ourselves as well as what we believe and intend for our world, yet it's still more than this. It's what we see and seek to see in that first moment when we make eye contact with another person. When it's positive, curious and accepting, people share with you the most amazing things. When you seek to see their inner turmoil, insight and journey and the beauty of it all, then they know you are looking and their inner selves speak to you. I find this often happens without conscious processing on the part of either person. The experience lies at the centre of discovering meaningful connection. It has the potential to unearth a grounding wave of calm and a sense of peace and enduring happiness.

IN OR OUT?

As humans, we do use judgments for well-intended reasons, too. We make judgments to show we are part of a particular group, sometimes by rejecting individuals from another group. This is something we needed to do in prehistoric times when threats and dangers meant that being part of a group equalled safety and a better chance of staying alive.

Take the fast-food example given earlier. If I decide fast food is bad I would be likely to inwardly, and probably outwardly, think and say negative things about people who eat a lot of fast food. In doing so, I become part of a group who see themselves as making better eating choices. The group is formed by criticizing people who eat more fast food, and the bonds are strengthened by the level of vigour and commitment that this criticism takes. The question is: Is being part of a group that is formed and bolstered by being critical of others who are "not like them" a happy place to be?

Groups formed through shared negative judgments of others carry a level of risk: you could be the target of criticism by the group at any point and move to being outside, rather than within, the inner circle. Fear of this weakens the chance for genuine constructive connections between the group members. We are familiar with the idea of the high-school "popular" group and what happens to the outsiders. What we often don't see is how we can act similarly, but on a low-level, daily basis without realizing it. Be vigilant for moments when you offer a negative judgment. If you do catch yourself, consider for a moment the broader ripples that may come from this.

Social psychologists study this behaviour through what is known as social identity theory, which looks at how people construct membership of groups, maintain them over time and the many and varied consequences of group behaviour. There are studies that show how groups form through focusing on their differences to other groups and the negative consequences this can bring. But it is also worth noticing other research, such as that by Tajfel and Turner in 2004, that show how groups can form in a more positive way and in their activities look for similarities and connections (not differences) with other groups. This second version is a more hopeful idea of groups, where the focus is on discovering shared interests and connecting to others rather than excluding them. It is an idea we teach children when we ask them to share, listen to others and not leave others out of play and games. It offers a way to be within a group without the focus being on exclusion. It is, again, a departure from negative judgment of others. These groups are arguably safer for their members as there is a fluidity to the identity of the members where alternative and other influences are of interest. You can be within the group, openly different and still accepted.

BEING PRESENT

Back to my work with Gyan. In the playroom, or maybe after my sessions, it slowly dawned on me that I was stuck in my own head. Before this point I felt quite self-assured that I could think and talk my way out of most things. And, to be honest, into most things, too, if that's where I was trying to be. The head place just didn't work here. It was as though Gyan knew I was thinking, anticipating and evaluating rather than just getting into the play. The focus on being only in my head created a block between us.

So, here was all this head stuff about intention from the programme leaders and yet, in a kind of contradictory fashion, it seemed to boil down to letting go of the thinking. Fortunately, I just had to get on and do it, be with him, totally absorbed in his world. Perhaps that's what most children need from their play companions and Gyan was no exception. Children love it when adults play without inhibition, immersed in the game, just as the children do themselves. By just playing and being fully committed to the playing, the head-focused stuff was released. I was present.

Words often got in the way of connected play, so I was left with my body and my senses. I learned to feel the walls and tap with specific spots on my hands as Gyan did. I learned to listen intently to the pace, intonation and volume of the sounds he made and re-create them. I learned to smell, pause and imagine as he did when aromas of Grandma's cooking drifted into his playroom. I learned to look at, stare and gaze into the details of fluff balls, dots on the wall, marks on the board and see the detail he saw. In short, I was using my senses.

At the start of these sessions, it felt foreign, embarrassing and uncomfortable. In time, though, it became more my therapy than his. Such playing made the stresses of life drift away. An escape into a more honest world. A world of sensing over thinking. I felt more present.

It was fascinating to discover that the way out of the anxiety in my mind was through awakening the senses and being more "in my body". This was hugely attractive to me as it was simple and more immediate than any talking therapy.

"IT WAS FASCINATING TO DISCOVER THAT THE WAY OUT OF THE ANXIETY IN MY MIND WAS THROUGH AWAKENING THE SENSES AND BEING MORE IN MY BODY"

These two lessons were so simple, yet so radical for me: releasing judgment and using all the senses to be present. Two decades on, it still astounds me how powerfully these two gems create connection.

More importantly, though, when I did this in the playroom the magic happened: Gyan responded. The whole point of our work was to build social connection for Gyan first. When we joined him in this immersive fashion we entered his world, came alongside him and made human connection as inviting to him as it can get. Imagine, a friend really seeing things from your viewpoint and totally wanting to do whatever you really enjoy, with you. That was who we wanted to be for him. We learned how to be that person for ourselves and for others in the process. Totally present and free of judgment. With you "as you are".

So, this book is simple – it explores being with you as you are in all different aspects of daily life. It's an exploration of being free of internal and external judgment. It's an antidote to the potential damage of social media and life within a competitive society, where comparison and its consequences are far too often the thieves of joy.

THE OPPOSITE OF SOMETHING

Sometimes exploring the opposite of something makes it easier to understand what it is. When I think about being fully immersed in being "as you are", this is the polar opposite to what's known as a deficit orientation.

The first time I read the phrase "deficit orientation", I re-read it then looked it up online. I tried to explain it several times to other people and by about the third time I got it! It's a complicated but wonderful phrase. So, here is my distilled and tested explanation of a deficit orientation:

An orientation is the direction in which we focus and what we are looking toward. A deficit is something missing, incorrect, at fault, something less than right.

So, what's the opposite of a deficit orientation?

Simply, it's focusing on what works, what's going well and how to build on it. It's not ignoring what isn't going so well. Instead, when we look at everything, we notice what's happening and focus on how to improve it. It's a big part of positive psychology, a domain of psychology founded by Martin Seligman. It sits alongside mindfulness to an extent, but it leans more toward positive judgment rather than a suspension of judgment. Positive psychology is radical. I find it liberating because, for me, it's a shift away from looking at mental health in terms of problems and difficulties and what's not working (often termed pathology). Instead, it encourages us to build and grow the aspects of human character that create happiness, freedom, connection and peace. Examining and addressing the pathology might still be useful, but essentially positive psychology says this is not the only way.

Seligman's work, which offers simple practices with great academic weight behind them, still rarely filters through to you and me, the everyday person. In this book we seek to demystify the work of academics and create something more accessible by distilling its essence and offering it through storytelling.

GET THE AS-YOU-ARE HABIT

How to approach this book

1 | WHERE FIRST?

Now that you have read this first chapter, dip into the rest of the book as suits you. You can think of the chapters as a group of short stories or essays that work in any order.

2 | MAKE IT YOURS

Consider the stories shared, and imagine how your own personal stories resonate with the themes. Perhaps even write down one of your own stories.

3 | TRY IT OUT

At the end of every chapter you will find a suggestion for how to create a habit or practice from the thinking offered. These first steps are accessible to everyone. Take note of these suggested habits and "have a go".

4 | NOTICE YOUR FEELINGS

Notice what happens to your feelings as you try the habit. Notice where each feeling sits within your body.

5 | NOTICE THE INNER CHATTER

Notice how the inner chatter of your mind responds. Does it change in pace? Does it change in content? Any other variations to what usually goes on for you?

6 | SHARE

Share what you have noticed with a friend or maybe even a stranger. Notice what happens for you when you share your experience. Notice what happens to your connection with this person.

COMPARISON IS
THE THIEF OF JOY

COMPARISON IS THE THIEF OF JOY

Feeling great about other people's brilliance

Ruth Williams | Department Store for the Mind

Personally, I find everything I do about self-acceptance works really well when I do it by myself. The existence of other people, however, makes it more tricky. For example, I can feel brilliant about my thick, unruly hair and the bushy character it brings until I encounter that super clean and tidy mum with her very long, apparently naturally blonde, smooth, silky hair, drifting like an unhurried angel across the playground. In that moment, comparison conducts a brutal and complete street-mugging of my previous sense of joy.

Social media puts a thickly intense magnifying glass over the impact of this experience. Every click, scroll and view offers something else I don't have, didn't think of and haven't done. There is a potential tidal wave of "life deficit" (things that are missing) realizations on offer for free with the feeds from all those well-known apps. It could be understood as FOMO ("fear of missing out"), but I would argue that it is this, but also something more.

The potentially crushing impact of comparison stretches across so much of life. School, work and socializing all require compliance with a certain level of look, behaviour and apparent ownership of things. Every encounter with others, real or digital, can become a reminder of what's missing.

This sense of deficit often has little to do with how much you own or earn. Some of the wealthiest people I have known, when sharing their true feelings over a glass of wine, will tell of missed opportunities or missing experiences with the same depth of pain as those who have never known wealth, and with

" "

IF A MAN DOES NOT
KEEP PACE WITH HIS
COMPANIONS, PERHAPS
IT IS BECAUSE HE
HEARS A DIFFERENT
DRUMMER. LET HIM
KEEP STEP TO THE
MUSIC WHICH HE
HEARS, HOWEVER
MEASURED OR
HOWEVER FAR AWAY.

Henry David Thoreau

whom I've had similar conversations. Could, perhaps, the wealthy feel it even more? Could that very experience of striving, which allowed them to create the wealth, be rooted in a deep fear of something missing? Of course, the psychotherapists would probably agree it was worth investigating. The monk, owning nothing other than the clothes on his back, sitting under the tree, would nod along, too. However, the question I am most interested in exploring here is: "How can we live an average day-to-day existence while preserving our sense of joy and building a solid shield against the theft that comparison can bring?"

DEALING WITH THE DIGITAL – WHAT LIES BENEATH?

To some extent, we tend to replicate whatever we do in real life within the digital world. The interesting part is to explore the difference between doing the thing in a digital environment and doing it in the real one. The classic difference that is often referred to is how the way we are distanced from what we do plays a part. When we are not physically with someone but commenting, tweeting or posting updates, we are more likely to do things we wouldn't do in person. We have that distance. The upside of this is the honesty it can elicit; the downside is the lessening of a sense of care, consideration or responsibility for the repercussions of what we do. How does this impact upon our experiences of comparison in relation to robbing our joy?

The distance in the digital environment takes away the wider context. Consider the beautiful mum in the playground, whom I mentioned at the start of this chapter, robbing me of my sense of joy about my hair. What actually happened is that when I looked at her she turned and smiled. Then, a few minutes later, I saw her struggling to control a toddler throwing a tantrum. The wider context was that she was friendly (the smile) and struggling with regular parenting challenges. This context made me feel connected to her, I saw more of the whole picture and, in doing so, I felt closer to her. She is just as human and perfectly imperfect as me. A single picture on Instagram, for instance, would not have given me such context.

Kristin Neff, a researcher and writer who spends her life exploring self-compassion, describes one of its three components as being a "common humanity" – a sense that we have a shared experience with others (see also Chapter 3, page 42). The opposite is a sense of isolation, that we are the only ones experiencing suffering. The wider context gives a sense of "common humanity". When consuming any edited digital information and imagery it's so important to reinsert the wider context using your imagination. Remind yourself that the food blogger might not have eaten the meal they photographed, that outside the frame of that beautiful lifestyle shot was probably untidy chaos and maybe a couple of dirty beer bottles or that the calm, insightful wisdom from the beautiful guru probably came from a lifetime of ups, downs and learning through mistakes. It's not about feeling good about ourselves by knocking other people. It's about feeling good about ourselves because we all present an edited slice of what we want people to see and that's just how it is. Comparing ourselves to the edited version as if it's the whole picture is a waste of time because you're comparing yourself to something that doesn't exist. I find it crucial to my own emotional survival to remind myself of this at least a dozen times a day. I love the way we edit and present ourselves to the world and, as a psychologist, I have a deep curiosity about what lies beneath. Imagining it makes me smile inside and allows a lightness to run through my life. Perhaps this is why observational comedy is such a great source of insight, because it nearly always deals with outing reality through humour.

"HOW CAN WE LIVE AN AVERAGE DAY-TO-DAY EXISTENCE WHILE PRESERVING OUR SENSE OF JOY AND BUILDING A SOLID SHIELD AGAINST THE THEFT THAT COMPARISON CAN BRING?"

It's all fake news. Recognizing that the feeds on social media are likely to be as selected and manipulated as any marketing or advertising activity is vital. We laugh at the messages adverts suggest: that we will be sexually attractive to everyone if we use a certain deodorant or that we will win the love of a lady by parachuting into her room with chocolates. We know this is not a true or complete picture of reality, so don't let your brain be tricked into thinking it is. You can choose what you believe; it might require a more concerted effort to remind yourself, but it's worth it and will potentially save you a lot of pain, distress and self-doubt.

DEALING WITH THE DIGITAL - TAKING CONTROL

Feeling out of control in any aspect of your life can bring you down. One way to understand depression is to think of it as feeling unhappy and being unable to change that unhappiness. Feeling in control is important to managing your emotions. In my opinion, there is nothing more sneaky at taking over, at this point in time, than the smartphone.

When I switched off all the notifications on my phone it was amazing. The smartphone no longer governed me. I chose when I looked at it and at what. I felt more relaxed. Taking back control felt good. I didn't miss anything important, either, which surprised me.

The digital-detox gurus out there encourage us to check our email only at specific times of the day, rather than at the moment it pings into our inbox. Some people even add a note to their signature to say that this is their approach. Others then know not to expect an instant response. Adopting a similar approach is a great way to take control and limit the constant interruptions, which can cause us so much stress.

Think before you look. Just ask yourself: What am I looking for? If it's not going to add to your sense of joy and happiness then perhaps, shock horror, put the phone down and do something else! It's so easy to find yourself accidentally flicking through the most mundane or unhelpful garbage for a hideously long time, only to find your mood brought down at the end.

I would advocate a little light goal-setting. Consider:

- What am I looking for?

- Why?

- What will trigger the end of this session on my phone?

The end part could be that you have found the answer to whatever it was you were looking for.

When we curate and control our use of the phone, then we make a measured choice about the sorts of information we absorb. We will consciously shape our influences and the sources of potential comparison we encounter. Personally, I like to aim to only spend time absorbing content that provides a fuller context. You could set your own criteria and test content against it to discover if it's working for you.

SELF-CARE – A BUFFER AGAINST COMPARISON

When we exercise self-compassion, then the things we observe about others become interesting details about the ways they are similar, different and just themselves. The interdependent connection that can create feelings of inadequacy between others' abilities, beauty and success and our own can be broken. It's just easier to do when we take care of ourselves.

If your sense of self is fragile, then it's far more vulnerable to the knocks comparison can bring.

Self-care is personal, and creating a self-care routine will probably be a journey of trial and error. However, the journey is likely to be fun. Next, I'll share my story of finding self-care through yoga; then I'd encourage you to take the time to discover what works for you.

If I was a car, then yoga would be my engine oil. However, just like car oil, there are many brands and types on offer and only a small handful that satisfactorily lubricate my parts. I've tried many different yoga classes with many different yoga teachers in many different surroundings. Rosie was warm, mumsy, overweight and struggled to demonstrate the positions but created a wonderfully nurturing environment. The Buddhist expert demonstrated yoga as a competitive sport and spent the class apparently showing off his incredible flexibility; unfortunately, none of the participants could manage what he demonstrated. On my yoga journey, I've discovered that Iyengar yoga is my favourite. The class I love the most is run by this amazing, unassuming woman who offers reduced rates for those working in the not-for-profit sector, on the top floor of a high-rise block overlooking the sea. I like the helpful little adjustments she provides and the focus on stretching only to your limit.

When I started this search I didn't know what I liked, or understand what was on offer in the world of yoga. Sometimes I felt intimidated, slipping back into comparison with other participants' abilities, and other times I felt at ease. What felt best was dedicating some time to finding out how best to take care of myself. That alone was invaluable.

> "WHEN WE CURATE AND CONTROL
> OUR USE OF THE PHONE, THEN WE MAKE
> A MEASURED CHOICE ABOUT THE SORTS
> OF INFORMATION WE ABSORB"

REAL TIME IN THE REAL WORLD

The editing that occurs online, spewing out a distorted slice of reality, can be found in our real-time day-to-day interactions in life, too, where our brains are the editors. As we saw in Chapter 1 (see page 12), our mental processing can only handle a limited amount of information, which means that when we encounter other people we make generalizations, draw conclusions and assume connections all the time, just to survive. It's not wrong, it's just necessary. However, such processing creates bias in our thinking. We can't stop it happening, but we can become more aware of it. By becoming aware of it, though, we can make more of a conscious choice about how we act in response to that bias in our thinking. It can be this very bias that leads us to make unhelpful comparisons based on limited information. By remembering there are layers of connection and complexity that go beyond the snapshot we have observed, we can begin to see the futility of comparison and the value of curiosity.

33

Here's a story to illustrate...

As part of my research for writing my contributions to this book, I interviewed Jackie Field (see Chapter 6, page 84). Before the interview I knew she was in her late thirties or early forties and that she had achieved some highly impressive results running marathons and competing in triathlons and Ironman events. That was about the extent of my prior knowledge. I'd arranged to interview her at home and arrived late one weekday morning. The house was set in its own acre of beautiful grounds, filled with trees, plants and a sloping lawn offering breathtaking views. The kitchen was large and filled with outdoor gear and musical instruments. In my mind, I decided Jackie had always been into fitness, would be competitive in all aspects of her life and had known wealth and little struggle. I felt somewhat intimidated by the prospect of interviewing her and needed to fight off waves of inadequacy, silencing my doubt-filled inner chatter. For every conclusion I drew about Jackie's success there was a corresponding dark thought lurking in the back of my mind about my own deficit.

"CHALLENGE YOURSELF TO SEE WHAT SOLID EVIDENCE YOU HAVE BASED YOUR CONCLUSIONS ON AND TEST ITS VALIDITY"

During the interview I discovered a tender human being, complete with many strengths and some self-doubt too. She shared how she and her husband had worked hard themselves, clearing the garden and breathing life back into the grounds, which had been quite neglected when they purchased the house. Jackie had started running only to combat postnatal depression and enjoyed the social side of taking part far more than any completion. She worked hard running three businesses while looking after two boys to earn the money they needed. In short, the reality challenged pretty much every conclusion I had inaccurately drawn. Her journey was filled with far more complex twists and turns then I had envisaged. She was just as imperfectly human as me and during the interview we formed a bond that I hope will be the start of a new friendship.

This story shows how the bias inherent in our thinking processes can not only lead to creating joy-thieving comparison, but also has the potential to steer us away from the path of friendship. When we feel intimidated by someone's success, we may not make that step to be our true selves with them and make friends.

Watch out for the bias that may creep into your thinking, and be what I'll call a "detective" when it does. Challenge yourself to see what solid evidence you have based your conclusions on and test its validity. An easy one to spot is when you decide you like or dislike new people. Explore, for a moment, why you feel like this and what triggered the response. Look for solid evidence again and be aware of bias. Investigate how you are comparing yourself, based on your conclusions, and what impact this is having on your interactions. I always find it helpful to remember that people always do the best they can in any situation based on what resources they have available to them. When you look for their available resources as a way to understand their behaviour, it often starts to make more sense.

HE GOES THE EXTRA MILE

Theft of joy at work is rife. Comparison is an ever-present beast in the majority of organizations. It happens because standards or criteria are set against which people are compared, and not only does this decide what sort of work they can do but also how much they get paid and how many perks they can access. Decidedly joyless!

Contemporary workplaces have begun to reject this way of working, because it both delivers a crushing blow to the levels of happiness and reduces productivity. This means less money for the owners, which is always a motivator to pay attention.

We work best when we have freedom to do the work, whatever it is, in the way that works for us, as the unique beings that we are. We work best when we feel valued for our individuality. We are more creative (nearly always good for the bottom line) when we can be ourselves rather than a robot-like copy of our colleagues.

We are more motivated in a way that is enduring over time when our rewards are based on the things we value, rather than external things that are applied to everyone in the same way (such as a financial bonus).

In short, comparison at work is not only the thief of joy, it is also the more traditional type of thief – it steals the cash.

If you are a boss, the central approach is to manage people by listening to them, encouraging them to see work as a place to discover and cultivate their individuality and creating space in your systems and processes to make this possible.

If you are an employee, then you can seek employers that do this, but you can also do plenty for yourself. Take time to discover who you are and how you like to work. For a start, you can discover your signature character strengths using the Resources provided at the back of this book (see page 156). Watch out for the little ways in which unhelpful comparison can creep in between you and the people you work with. Challenge your thinking when it does and maybe even that of your colleagues, when appropriate. Share who you are with your line manager and how you work best. Be creative and suggest ways in which you can think about and adapt your work to play to these strengths. Even if the current culture isn't quite there yet, you may slowly start a revolution from within. Good luck!

GET THE NO-COMPARE HABIT

Ways to preserve your sense of joy

1 | NOTICE THE NOW

As you go about your daily life just notice when you make comparisons between yourself and others. Notice what happens to your feelings, body and thoughts when you do.

2 | START SMALL

Choose one of the moments of comparison and explore how accurate your assumptions were. What were the facts? How does this shape your impression and subsequent comparison?

3 | REINSERT THE CONTEXT

Digital information is usually edited to create an appearance of something. Always remember to reinsert the wider context by imagining what is happening outside the image or soundbite.

4 | COMMON HUMANITY

We all struggle, suffer and feel joy. Whatever you are feeling, others in this world will be sharing that same experience at the same time. Notice how reminding yourself of this affects your feelings.

5 | SELF-CARE

Make time to do things that increase your sense of peace and joy. The more these things encourage you toward accepting all the different layers of yourself, the better.

6 | QUESTION

Remember we all do the best we can with the resources we have available. Question the need to compare and steer yourself more toward curious observation whenever you can.

CHAPTER 3

IT'S NOT PINK
AND IT WAS
NEVER FLUFFY

IT'S NOT PINK AND IT WAS NEVER FLUFFY

The strength in looking after yourself

Ruth Williams | Department Store for the Mind

"We don't do all that pink fluffy stuff," I was told yet again by the mostly male science and technology delegates attending one of my leadership skills training courses. Throughout the next three days I felt confident that at least some of them, hopefully all, would begin to realize that the "pink fluffy stuff" they were referring to would provide them with greater resilience, influence and leadership potential. This was a relatively extreme experience of how people often find it awkward talking about emotions, self-care or self-compassion. The terminology sounds and feels personal, perhaps invasive, and a likely precursor to a requirement to disclose our inner emotional selves. The more we have hidden our emotions, the more we are likely to feel those uncomfortable sensations. Taking time to care for our emotional selves, we may fear, could also suggest a mental-health concern, and few of us feel comfortable talking about any mental health-issues we may have. But if we could feel as at ease talking about the benefits to our mental wellbeing of a self-care routine as we do about the benefits to our bodies of going for a run, then the more likely we would all be to get involved.

The thinking we shared on this training course was about developing the peace within ourselves so that we are able to listen to and understand others. The strength to do this comes from knowing, accepting and caring for yourself rather than seeing yourself as having worth in comparison to others. This is one way of understanding the difference between self-compassion and self-esteem. The reason why the self-compassionate approach is often stronger and more enduring is because it exists independently of others. Self-esteem

" "

THE WOMAN WHO
DOES NOT REQUIRE
VALIDATION FROM
ANYONE IS THE MOST
FEARED INDIVIDUAL
ON THE PLANET

Mohadesa Najumi, writer and social scientist

usually focuses more on how you perceive your worth, and arguably worth and value are relative measurements – these require comparison on some form of scale and rely on how esteemed you view yourself to be, in comparison to others. Self-compassion and self-care, on the other hand, do not rely on comparison to others and sit within your heart, within your very sense of being. This approach doesn't make you angry or want to fight to prove that your way is the right way, because it values difference and different opinion. It does, however, give you the strength to hold your ground with individuality and integrity.

Self-compassion researcher and writer Kristin Neff identifies the ability to take care of yourself during times of emotional suffering as an important component of self-compassion. If you can do this, you can risk emotional suffering and survive it. You have the skills you need to weather the storm: certain habits or rituals tailored to you that are concerned with taking care of your emotional and your physical self. These self-care rituals can be simply sharing a drink with friends after a day at the office, or regularly practising mindfulness throughout the working week.

Nearly every person attending my three-day leadership courses would comment at some point about how brilliant it was to hear from other leaders that they were experiencing the same challenges. This would so often be followed by comments about how they thought they were the only ones. I'd like to say my training was the most valuable part, but I actually think that this collective experience and the relationships it created filled that role. These supportive friendships continued long after the course, reminding those leaders who took part that they were not alone.

The value of not feeling alone or isolated cannot be underestimated. We gain strength, confidence and peace from feeling others experience the things we do. We create a network of support and a means to access advice by sharing our own suffering, however large or small. People in leadership positions need this as much as anyone else, and the people I worked with, mostly first-line managers, needed it more than anyone. They "got it in the neck" from both their team members and their own line managers. However, they were only on the first step in the leadership ladder and they had little influence. Throw into this challenging mix the fact that most of them were new to the job, with no prior experience, and we have a group of people in dire need of support. Spending time establishing that sense of community and reminding yourself you are not alone is a crucial part of self-care. This might mean that a drink with friends can be as healing as a meditation session.

"FEEL, RECOGNIZE AND ACCEPT OUR OWN EMOTIONS WITHOUT BEING DOMINATED BY THEM"

The application of mindfulness within organizations has become increasingly popular over the last decade. For me, this means developing the skills to accept and understand the emotions we feel without becoming overwhelmed by them. It conjures images of great leaders who could continue to think calmly and make decisions wisely during crisis or battle. The vast majority of us crave the capacity to do this – to feel, recognize and accept our own emotions without being dominated by them. My participants, in their leadership roles, needed it deeply. They often had to manage their own emotional experience so they could lead calmly and with conviction. They were regularly required to sit one-to-one with people who were sharing a rollercoaster of emotions with them, without diving into the same unsteadying ups and downs. It's no wonder that mindfulness is spreading through organizations like wildfire.

DRAWING THE LINE
Self-compassion can build the strength in men and women to establish boundaries and, in doing so, not only protect themselves but also create a life within which they can discover more about who they are. Dysfunctional family experiences in early life can make setting boundaries tricky, but not impossible. Learning to treat yourself with compassion and care will help you to get to know and appreciate more fully who you are, and to build the strength and confidence to set boundaries, to know what treatment you want, expect and deserve from others around you. This creates a positive cycle: the lines drawn define more clearly your understanding of self and simultaneously protect you

" "

GROWING
SELF-COMPASSION
RATHER THAN
BUILDING
SELF-ESTEEM

from potentially mistreating others (when we know how we want to be treated, we can apply the same treatment to those around us). At the heart of this positive cycle we find the skills to articulate to others – with firm, steadfast kindness – where our boundaries lie.

I was a teenager in the late 1980s and early 1990s. Attitudes to sexual assault were arguably quite different back then, as can be seen through the recent exposé of well-known figures. For women, the setting of boundaries arguably required some attention during this period, but at the same time, many men and boys were guided by social influences in a way I am sure many regret today. I attended an all-girls, relatively rough school. Around the age of 15 and 16, a lot of the girls started to lose their virginity. When someone came in with gossip or shared a story themselves, the question asked in response was too often: "Did she want to or did he force her?" The girls did not flinch in asking. I could tell more than a dozen stories of assault and rape of girls I knew at that age. No one thought for a moment about reporting it to the police. It shocks me to my core now to think of it! How did we think that was OK?

Behind a wall of silenced shame, I believe we will discover many boys and men who were sexually active during this time and behaved in ways that they deeply wish they could change. Yet when we care for ourselves and learn to tend kindly to our own emotions, we often develop the skills and motivation to do the same for others. From this position, we would not hurt others sexually or emotionally. Shame creates a huge barrier to self-care.

Let me take this to a more moderate level for a moment and share a story of working in the finance industry. This was a part-time job and I was recruited by a friend who was the interim managing director of an office of a global organization. The dozen or so employees were all men, except for me. I found the culture competitive and unkind. They didn't trust each other and although they'd drink together at lunchtime, they would all tell me awful tales of misdemeanours about one another "on the quiet". This was my first experience of the finance industry's culture and it was the early Noughties. The MD, after a few months, didn't work out, and the trader asked to step into his position had been giving me lurid looks since I'd started. Now the comments came along with the slight and frequent invasions of my personal space. I'm tall and could physically hold my ground. I didn't show fear and whenever a comment such as "Oh, look at that – sexy legs and she has a brain" was uttered, I would pause, look him in the eye and continue unflustered without responding. It niggles me still now, though, that I didn't do anything more than resign from my position. Could things have been different if I'd worked on my self-care and self-compassion? Would the outcome have changed if I had worked on building the confidence to set boundaries, to know how I deserved to be treated?

Yes, that slimy toad would have been told in the meeting by me, without hesitation, that his comment was inappropriate and unprofessional. I would have explained how it made me feel, in front of the whole management team, and I would have asked for an immediate apology. Perhaps I would even have asked for the opinion of others in the room about whether we needed to agree some ground rules concerning how we treat one another as we "clearly didn't share the same understanding". It's great to dream of that now.

"DEVELOPING THE PEACE WITHIN OURSELVES
SO WE ARE ABLE TO LISTEN TO AND
UNDERSTAND OTHERS."

How many men and women reading this will have been harassed at work like me? How many will have felt fear? Far too many. This is not to say that the by focusing on self-compassion and setting boundaries we can prevent and end all harassment. But by caring for ourselves and growing in our confidence to establish these boundaries we are going some way to tending our world, to changing attitudes and behaviour.

Now, it's different attitudes again that come into play. What, for instance, is porn doing to the new generation of teenage girls and boys? A friend who runs sex-education classes with teens recently shared with me that a lot of her work is about educating teenagers that sex is not like porn. Call me old-fashioned but that feels like a hard knock back to the Dark Ages, if our more emotionally

literate, environmentally aware young adults are seeing porn role models as the way to treat one another during sex. Surely a self-compassionate teen would not put themselves, or anyone else, in that position? Perhaps during these turbulent teenage years, we most need to learn the skills of self-care and self-compassion to ensure we create a positive cycle for ourselves that enables us to establish boundaries. For parents of teenagers riding the waves of fun and danger as they test out the world around them, the skills of calm, present, non-judgmental listening are never more challenged or required.

Feeling part of and connected to humanity, rather than isolated and alone, is crucial for both teenagers at risk of making mistakes and people who have experienced assault. Look at what happens when a few come forward, as they did through the #MeToo movement in 2017. The knowledge that they are not alone in their suffering gives many the confidence to share their stories, too. The perpetrator's power, which stems from creating a sense of isolation in their victims, can be crushed with a formidable force when we remember, with conviction, that we are not alone in our suffering. That calm, present, non-judgmental listening by a parent provides the chance to save their teenager from the danger of feeling alone. The more we can listen like this to both ourselves and others, the more we can make constructive choices.

THE STRENGTH OF A ROLE

I've grown in confidence over the years since I worked in the finance industry and have shaped a career through speaking truth to power as a business psychologist. That power is usually in the hands of older men. However, it's far easier to speak this truth when you have an appointed role. When that role needs to be defined from within and is not validated from outside, then inner strength is needed.

So, how do you create a role for yourself that gives you permission to establish boundaries, say no when it feels right for you to do so and ask for the things that you need? Working on the skills of self-compassion and self-care, and the exercises that help develop these, can build the strength within to establish boundaries. There are also other approaches that you can draw upon. I used to teach a drama technique to help people develop presentation skills, and this exercise can work for anyone. First, you have to create a persona for a strong woman who speaks her mind with firm kindness and self-compassion. When you have this character created in your mind, you can "put her on" and try her out. Imagine the way she stands, the words she uses and the response she receives. When your posture is upright and your chin is raised, you can make eye contact more easily. When you do this, the way you breathe and project your voice changes. Try it out and see how it feels in your body. You can discover exercises and thoughts on how to work on the relationship between posture and voice in *The Voice Book* (see page 154).

"SELF-COMPASSION BUILDS STRONG, TENACIOUS LEADERS WHO EMBRACE CHALLENGE."

Returning to our strong woman, she is clear in her meaning. She uses short sentences and does not apologize for her feelings. Her language is definite, not tentative. She is steady in her pace and pauses with ease between the points she makes. Her face is relaxed, and she is at ease enough to smile when it fits in with what she is saying. Now imagine inserting yourself in all these aspects. Mix the ideas with your own personal ways of being and with your turns of phrase. Play scenarios out in your mind of how she would respond to your day-to-day activities. You can even use physical creativity – drawing or painting how she looks or writing down a journal entry for her typical day – to help breathe life into her.

The magic happens when people apply this exercise to improving their presentation skills. It comes about through the responses they receive. Because their audience perceives them as relaxed and confident, they smile back, listen attentively and engage. The speaker responds in kind and the interaction between them convinces the audience further of the value of this character. Typically, this interaction means the speaker relaxes, draws on more of their true self and naturally becomes the character they had been playing. The play-acting is temporary, because it soon initiates an interaction with the audience that resolves most confidence issues. Of course, this may not work every time, but it is an example of the powerful value of creating a character and role for yourself that it is worth being aware of. We cannot control the response of an audience or another person, but we can control how we behave. And how we behave will shape the response we receive. We always have a choice.

THE GENTLE MIGHT OF SELF-COMPASSION

The action to establish boundaries, then, stems from accepting oneself and making a commitment to take care of one's own emotions. From this position, boundaries are established, not with aggression but with a kind and firm approach. This action need not come from a place of anger because we can develop the capacity to recognize and manage our emotions. When we need to establish a boundary, we will then not be overwhelmed by the fear and anger we may feel. Because of this, we do not meet the bullish dominator with their own tactics. Instead we have something far stronger, because it comes from an honest place with a constructive purpose. The bull will sense this and crumble, at least a little, inside. At best they will be inspired and will share their own fear, too. After all, bullying behaviour nearly always stems from a place of fear and insecurity. This powerful might comes from the kind and gentle act of caring for oneself. It creates within a capacity to pay deep, tender attention to others and understand them more fully – the essence of effective leadership. This foundation of self-compassion builds strong, tenacious leaders who embrace challenge. Such people have an enduring mental resilience that depends upon their respect for the "pink fluffy stuff" inside us all.

GETTING THE PINK-POWER HABIT

First steps in self-care

1 | NOTICE
Notice how you feel in different situations, observing what scenarios lower your sense of self and which ones give you a lift.

2 | DETECT
Be a detective – notice what it is about these scenarios that creates different moods.

3 | CHOOSE
Look for other choices you can make in the scenarios that leave you feeling low.

4 | CONNECT
Notice when you feel isolated, as if you are the only one having that experience. Challenge your thinking to discover whether it's likely others are feeling the same.

5 | RELAX
Choose one mindful activity, using the Resources at the back of this book (see page 156), to introduce yourself to letting a little more peace creep in.

CHAPTER 4

STRONG STUFF

STRONG STUFF

A daily dose of playing to your strengths

Ruth Williams | Department Store for the Mind

"I'm getting healthy this year," says a good friend in early January.

What runs through your head?

Perhaps: "That's a good idea? Maybe I'll do a bit of the same? We could start a regular weekend walk together?"

Another day, another friend says, "I'm working on my mental health this year."

What runs through your head this time?

Perhaps: "Are they OK? They'll probably need some support? I hope they're not going to do anything to hurt themselves? I'll need to be careful about what I say around them now?"

Most of us tend to respond in this way. We tend to think of getting healthy overall as finding ways to be stronger and fitter. To discover sporting activities we enjoy, healthy foods we like to eat and finding ways to do more of both. It's a bit different when the question of mental health comes up. We then tend to assume that there's a problem, something in crisis, and check to ensure the person is working on finding out all they can about what that problem is and how to fix it. It's interesting to explore how thinking about mental health in the same ways that we tend to view physical health might bring change. What if we looked to find a way to discover and build on what we enjoy, what brings us happiness and fills us with confidence and a sense of self-worth?

" "

RATHER THAN
SEARCHING FOR
PROBLEMS AND
DYSFUNCTION WITHIN
OUR MINDS AND HOW
TO FIX IT, WE IDENTIFY
WHAT IS WORKING AND
HOW TO MAKE THE
MOST OF THAT

Which one of these approaches is more inviting? Which one would make you feel motivated, positive and perhaps even excited about doing something about it?

The resounding answer would be the "overall health" approach, rather than the typical "mental health" one. Very few of us, particularly when in a low and wobbly place, feel enthusiastic about spending a lot of time and energy finding out what's wrong with us and how we think about the world.

POSITIVE PSYCHOLOGY VERSUS THE THERAPIST'S COUCH

According to the founders of positive psychology, Martin Seligman and Mihalyi Csikszentmihalyi, "a science of positive subjective experience, positive individual traits, and positive institutions promises to improve quality of life and prevent the pathologies that arise when life is barren and meaningless".

In the latter part of the last century psychologists started exploring another way to imagine working on mental health. It falls under a part of the discipline of psychology called "positive psychology". I was so excited when I came across it as part of my studies, a couple of decades ago. I was excited because I thought "Wow, this could really work!" And not just for people experiencing some real challenges in their life, but for the everyday person who is seeking greater satisfaction, peace and happiness, too.

Positive psychology offers something different from the usual therapeutic adventures into the mind. Counselling, therapy and similar activities that often involve sitting in a small room with a gently probing, note-taking professional evoke a wave of dread in many of us. It can feel exposing. It can be scary to imagine that all those thoughts you never shared might suddenly be seen and judged. The commonly believed history of this sort of intervention suggests "issues" will be found, errors unearthed, mistakes of judgment openly voiced and a distinct lack of "normal function" identified. Many of us have spent a long time, perhaps a lifetime, dedicated to appearing as "normal" as possible. No wonder we are not drawn to the traditional counsellor's couch of old.

Positive psychology is an exciting alternative to this set-up. Perhaps you will still be one-to-one in a small room, but with positive psychology the questions you're asked will be about finding out what makes you tick. What puts you into that zone where you forget about everything else and are totally absorbed in the activity? What do you love? How can we create more of this in your life?

> "VERY FEW OF US, PARTICULARLY WHEN IN A LOW AND WOBBLY PLACE, FEEL ENTHUSIASTIC ABOUT SPENDING A LOT OF TIME AND ENERGY FINDING OUT WHAT'S WRONG WITH US AND HOW WE THINK ABOUT THE WORLD"

The principles are simple. Rather than searching for problems and dysfunction within our minds and how to fix them, we identify what is working and how to make the most of that. This doesn't mean we ignore the problems or discount the many amazing therapies that help support people in need. It does mean, though, that we begin from a place of strength and build. Not so scary after all.

The potential was tantalizing: I could see that this approach could reach huge numbers of people. People who might otherwise have hesitated in exploring the mind might be more willing if they knew their dark places were not to be probed as the main function of the activity. Healthier minds and debates about how to grow and nourish them could more readily become part of the daily debate for the average person. In the last three or four decades this swing has arguably affected the mainstream discussion. Today, for instance, you can barely watch a news programme without some mention of mental wellbeing – arguably the new and more comfortable way of referring to the mental health of the reasonably well masses.

TAKING THE PAIN OUT OF SCHOOL
School can be a great example of positive psychology in action. Typically, teachers report back to parents on how children have or have not met the standards expected for their age. It's often a retrospective look at the year, a story of what has happened so far. Time and energy are often spent on reporting the child's recent history so that an accurate judgment can be made.

CHARACTER STRENGTHS

If you focus on your strengths, they will grow. These 24 character strengths are based on the work of the VIA (Values in Action) Institute, which represents the most significant effort in history to review, assemble, research and classify the best qualities in human beings.

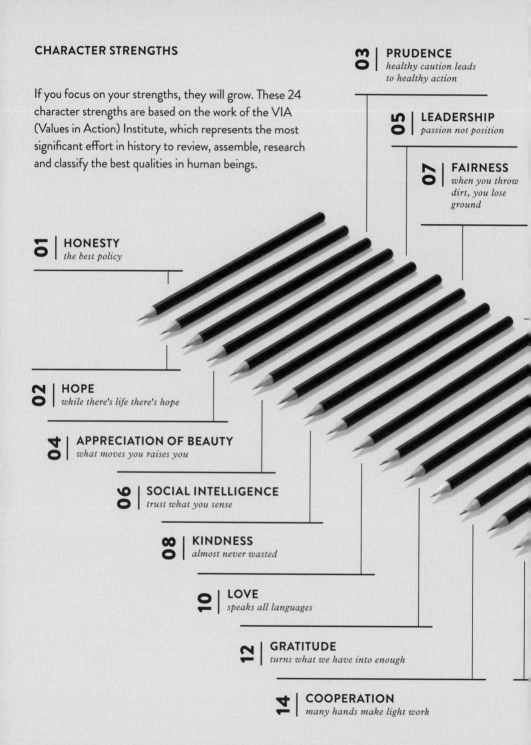

03 | PRUDENCE
healthy caution leads to healthy action

05 | LEADERSHIP
passion not position

07 | FAIRNESS
when you throw dirt, you lose ground

01 | HONESTY
the best policy

02 | HOPE
while there's life there's hope

04 | APPRECIATION OF BEAUTY
what moves you raises you

06 | SOCIAL INTELLIGENCE
trust what you sense

08 | KINDNESS
almost never wasted

10 | LOVE
speaks all languages

12 | GRATITUDE
turns what we have into enough

14 | COOPERATION
many hands make light work

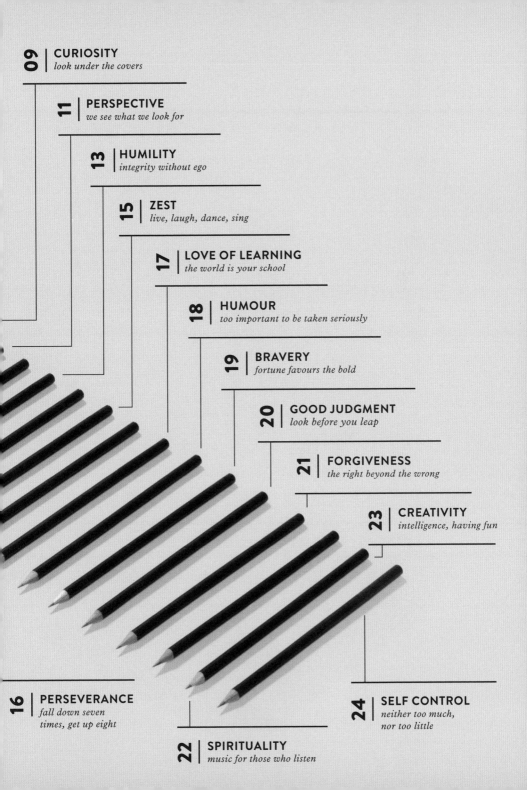

09 | CURIOSITY
look under the covers

11 | PERSPECTIVE
we see what we look for

13 | HUMILITY
integrity without ego

15 | ZEST
live, laugh, dance, sing

17 | LOVE OF LEARNING
the world is your school

18 | HUMOUR
too important to be taken seriously

19 | BRAVERY
fortune favours the bold

20 | GOOD JUDGMENT
look before you leap

21 | FORGIVENESS
the right beyond the wrong

23 | CREATIVITY
intelligence, having fun

16 | PERSEVERANCE
*fall down seven
times, get up eight*

22 | SPIRITUALITY
music for those who listen

24 | SELF CONTROL
*neither too much,
nor too little*

" "

THE MORE YOU
UNDERSTAND
AND ACCEPT
ABOUT YOURSELF,
THE MORE YOU
CAN GROW IN A
DIRECTION THAT
WORKS FOR YOU

What if, instead, we spent that time hearing from the teachers about what they had discovered about how each individual child learns? What if we spent that teacher–parent time planning together how home and school could shape the way future learning happened for the child? What if the aim was to work together as "learning detectives" to create an ever-evolving plan that shaped any subject which that child enjoyed and felt motivated to do? If we did, these are the sort of things we might hear in those meetings:

"Joe likes to doodle in his notebook when listening. Sometimes he writes down the things I say, sometimes the drawing is abstract. I've noticed that if he can have his notebook with him, he can listen for longer and tends to remember more."

"Cole needs time to chat about the things we learn with his friends and an adult for it to truly sink in. He has loads of questions but doesn't often like to ask them in the class. After each learning session we make a time to chat. It's amazing how much he remembers once we have done this. The chat needs to be at his pace."

"Sarah needs time outside for at least ten minutes in every hour to maintain concentration during the school day. We keep the doors open, so she can go and get a breath of fresh air whenever she needs to."

"Katie needs to create pictures and diagrams of the things we learn rather than write notes. We provide her with large sheets of paper, plenty of space and coloured pens so she can do this. Sometimes we put the posters she creates on the walls as they are a beautiful reminder of the key things we talked about."

"Jenny finds creating stories by writing them down frustrating, so she uses speech-activated software on the computer. Her creativity and imagination when she creates stories in this way are astonishing."

You may recognize some of these approaches as things great teachers do in supportive schools when children have been identified as "having problems". What might happen if all children were able to shape the way they learned like this?

WORKING FOR YOU

In adult life, research shows that people's performance in the workplace is considerably improved when they feel happier. People feel happier when they can approach the work they do with flexibility. If this flexibility gives them space to approach things in a way that works for them, they are happier and perform better. This sort of activity has a direct result on the bottom line (how much money an organization can make). The argument for the management team, when a clear financial benefit is in sight, becomes compelling and whatever is needed is more likely to be put in place to make it happen. As children's learning has no immediate financial impact, these practices can take longer to filter through to schools. This sort of change has a cost implication for schools, too. However, positive psychology approaches are still applied in places. Let's hope the practice spreads.

YOUR STRENGTHS AREN'T NECESSARILY WHAT YOU DO WELL

It all begins with finding out what you enjoy. This is not necessarily what you do better than other people. Out in the world are many unhappy individuals performing very highly in jobs they hate. Perhaps they trained hard in a particular profession, because it was expected of them. Perhaps they were told at school that this is where they got their highest test scores, so this is what they should do. Perhaps they were accidentally educated by their parents to be knowledgeable in a particular area, by happy (or unhappy) accident of this being their parents' profession. The reasons can be many. Sometimes these accidents work out and what you are good at is also what makes you happy. Often, they don't, and at a point in life a re-evaluation begins for those who have the opportunity and belief that they can effect a change.

Even if you are in a job you enjoy and generally feel satisfied with your work, understanding your strengths is still beneficial. The more you understand and accept about yourself, the more you can grow in a direction that works for you. There is a tendency to focus on developing areas of low performance but it is just as important to develop areas of average performance. We could argue that it's even more important to invest in this stage, because then you have the energy and the impetus to take things further. If we relate this

to the school example, earlier, it means giving the same attention to the mid- and high-performing students as you do to the lower-performing ones. In a work situation, this is an area of great debate and interest because of the bottom-line implications. If a management team spends all its time dealing with low performance and fire-fighting problems, then the valuable mid- and high-performers may become ignored. This could mean a drop in output and a loss of cash. Again, in business the argument is clear. So, not only are strengths worth reviewing when everything's OK, they can become a crucial part of getting the most out of life when you are in a good place, too. The whole idea of positive psychology is about growing rather than problem-solving and spotting mistakes, which means it's always relevant and you can turn to it at any time.

STRENGTHS – FIND THE BEASTS AND FEED THEM

You can discover strengths through personal reflection, by completing questionnaires such as the Values In Action (VIA, see page 156) and by working with a positive psychology professional. Perhaps a combination of all three might shed the most light. Whichever method works for you, it will be time well spent. Once you discover your strengths you can begin shaping the little and large parts of life so that you have more opportunity to use them.

Reflections around positive psychology involve noticing what makes you feel happy. Consider a time when you were so immersed in what you were doing that you experienced a sense of the rest of the world disappearing.

To put the idea of strengths into action I will share with you one strength I have noticed through reflection and one I have learned about through using the VIA survey.

The question ran through my head, "When do I feel most in that zone, that 'flow' state, where the world disappears and I'm immersed in what I'm doing?" Dancing! Not following the steps of a particular dance such as a salsa or learning a routine, but being on the dancefloor in a reasonably dark club where I am truly, to quote that disco classic from Sister Sledge, "Lost in Music". A dear friend, when watching a particularly unusual contemporary dance performance on TV with me, said, "That's a bit like how you dance." So, maybe it's not something I'm very good at, but who cares? There is something deeply satisfying for me about being able to "dance likes nobody's watching". Dancing is a strength for me and something I need to do regularly to feel balanced, for want of a better word.

> "DANCING IS A STRENGTH FOR ME AND SOMETHING I NEED TO DO REGULARLY TO FEEL BALANCED, FOR WANT OF A BETTER WORD."

I've spent considerable time trying to work out why dancing is so important to me, and I think I've cracked it. As a psychologist, I spend a lot of time and energy thinking about things in what aims to be a logical and objective way. That said, I have a strong tendency to overthink things, and dancing brings me back to my body. The way this happens is that it puts my consciousness back in my body and draws it away from my head. For me, if I try to think about what I'm doing when I dance, my feet become heavy and clumsy and the rhythm eludes me. If I relax into the music and let it all go, then it comes naturally and I am away. To keep the head part switched off, I try to forget that anyone else is there. If the music is loud enough, then talking isn't possible. Switching off the verbal option is good for me. So, dancing isn't one of the strengths you will find in the VIA survey, but finding time to be in my body versus my mind is a strength for me.

As a teen, in my twenties and even into my early thirties I danced often, finding club nights I really enjoyed and going out with people who would be happy just to dance for hours. As I became older, with longer working hours and less energy or less inclination to stay out until the early hours, I needed to be inventive. So, working from home at the time, when a friend left a large sound system in my care as they went off travelling, I started taking "dance breaks". Rather than sitting down with a coffee at intervals, away from the desk, I would instead turn up the volume and leap around like a loon to something with a great baseline. It did wonders for my energy and creativity. In a later chapter in life, as a busy mum, it got tricky again to find the time to dance. I missed it with

65

an almost bodily ache. Then the easiest solution dawned upon me: to introduce it as a regular thing at home with my two boys. They love it and even set up their own "disco" without me whenever they can. It's great exercise, incredibly funny and fills my need to get back in my body. Sometimes as life progresses you need to be more inventive to create moments to feed your strengths. It's time well spent.

A love of learning is one of my strengths identified by the VIA. It is one of my top five too, probably my strongest. There are twenty-four in total. Thinking back through my own story, this one has played a part in big and small ways from my earliest days. The smaller ones are some of the most interesting.

The bit about learning that I love most is seeing or being a part of that "eureka moment" for others, or creating the conditions to make the same happen for me. That moment of realization. The great stuff, the stuff of satisfaction, for me, is in the way a tiny piece of the puzzle clicking into place can open up a whole new way of thinking. If I'm getting deep, this tiny click, for me, is the whole reason why we are here. The tiny clicks are little points of individual evolution. There is nothing so obviously constant in the history of our world as continuous evolution. Moving evolution in a positive and constructive direction, I believe, is arguably our main reason for existence. Depending on your leaning, this can be linked to something more spiritual or not. So, being a part of shaping one person's understanding and realization about something becomes the purpose of being alive and part of humanity. Drawing this into my consciousness means I can use it to find enjoyment in life. By knowing that I love being a part of learning I am motivated to actively seek chances to learn and teach. When I do this, I feel energized. I also know that things stick in my head, become solidified in my memory, when I debate them with or explain them to others. Knowing that this is one of my strengths allows me to draw on it as a means to remember, a way to shape my work and something to turn to when I need a boost.

GET THE STRENGTHS HABIT

Ideas for spotting your strengths and playing to them

1 | REFLECT
Reflect on when you find yourself so involved in and enjoying an activity that the rest of the world and maybe even your worries seem to disappear out of your consciousness.

2 | DISCOVER YOU
Complete the VIA character questionnaire (see the Resources section at the back of this book, page 156) to discover your signature strengths.

3 | STRENGTH IN LIFE
Consider how your signature strengths play a part in the activity you reflected on at stage 1, as well as in other activities that you have enjoyed throughout your life.

4 | STRENGTH IN CHOICE
Notice how your signature strengths shape your approach to the world. Consider what you are drawn to and how you make decisions.

5 | SHAPING
Look for opportunities to shape the things you do daily in a way that allows you to use your signature strengths.

6 | NOTICE CHANGE
Notice how you feel in both body and mind when you incorporate more of your strengths into your daily life.

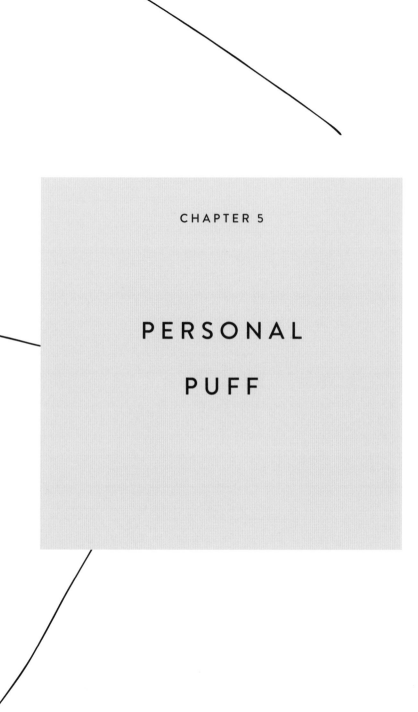

CHAPTER 5

PERSONAL

PUFF

CHAPTER 5

PERSONAL PUFF

We breathe differently. We can breathe consciously.

Aimee Hartley | The Breathing Room

My first-ever breath was on Saturday 23 November 1974 at 3.30am. According to my mum, it was a quiet breath but a strong one at least. Two years later, I very nearly took my last, as a nasty bout of croup made it difficult for me to catch a full breath, turning my face blue and my mum's a whiter shade of pale. Luckily my mum raced me to the hospital and, following a few days of intensive care, the colour returned to my cheeks and my breath returned fully to my body.

Later on, in my teenage years, I realized how out of breath I became when running. At school, I would drag myself around the muddy track, wheezing as others glided past me with effortless ease. Soon afterward, a prescribed inhaler became my reluctant running companion. Winter exercise felt like a "frenemy" (good for the heart, hard on my lungs) and I later learned that muddy fields are only ever fun at festivals.

Still in my teens, I thought it would be a great idea to start smoking. I didn't much like how it made me feel, but soon found myself addicted. Back in the day when smoking was often seen as a sociable, cool activity, and you could smoke anywhere – in cafés, pubs, clubs and even on buses and planes – the health hazards of smoking only appeared in small print, tiny enough to ignore. A few years on, though, my skin was pallid, my exercise routine a struggle and my energy levels at an all-time low.

Fortunately, in my late twenties, a big penny dropped when a strong and bossy voice inside me shouted: "You've got to look after yourself. Go and find a yoga course!" For once, I listened to my intuition and trusted it enough to act upon it.

" "

YOU TEACH
BEST WHAT YOU
MOST NEED
TO LEARN

Richard Bach

I never intended to become a yoga teacher, immersing myself on that first course purely to keep myself away from a build-up of unhealthy habits. Four years and two yoga courses later, the last one being a full-time yoga course in Australia, where I had to rise at 5am on a daily basis to practise breathing exercises, I was a full-time yoga junkie, certified yoga teacher and holding weekly classes back home in London. Yet even though a teacher and an avid practitioner, I still found it difficult to stay "present" in some of the poses, and certain poses even made me anxious – not a great way to feel, especially when you are teaching yoga.

"I WAS IN AWE OF THE POWER OF SIMPLY BREATHING IN THIS NEW, DEEPER WAY"

In the same studio where I held my classes there happened to be a "transformational breath" coach visiting; his posters suggested this technique could make me feel calm and more present in just one session. I signed up. Ninety minutes later, I felt like I had never felt before. I just wanted to stay there, lying in this awareness of brand-new human feelings, physical tingling, emotional waves of euphoria and a complete presence of mind. These sensations lasted for a few days and I was in awe of the power of simply breathing in this new, deeper way.

Throughout the session, my attention was solely on my breath, clocking each inhale and exhale. It felt like my mind was a pendulum simply swinging to and fro with each breath. I had a sense of moving from my usual busy headspace (always dreaming of the future or reminiscing about the past) to shifting to simply focusing on my belly rising and falling. Being curious about all the sensations my breath gave my body, I began using this new deep, belly breath to anchor my mind. I was, for the first time ever, really witnessing a new landscape – my deep diaphragmatic breath space, which was vast, boundless and free. My entire respiratory system felt open and expansive and my body and mind followed on. Feelings of ecstasy collided with deep sensations of calm. Only interrupted by my intuition telling me, in a slightly less bossy tone and with more conviction, to learn how to teach this incredible technique.

Transformational breathing combines conscious breathing, acupressure, sound and movement. It focuses primarily on bringing our awareness away from our thoughts and toward how we breathe and how this has an effect on how we feel.

A SUBTLE, SILENT POWER

We breathe, on average, 20,000 times a day – that's roughly seven million breaths a year – most of which pass us by unnoticed.

If anything else was happening to us, say sneezing or coughing 20,000 times a day, and suddenly we stopped, I'm sure we would notice the pause. The breath is so subtle, often a silent, invisible affair, that it's no wonder that so many breaths sneak by without a sound, like passing clouds. Our mind is a busy place, with more thoughts than breaths happening in our conscious brain. It's not surprising that we focus on our headspace, while our breath goes unnoticed. However, if we bring our mind's awareness to our breath, engaging in how the body feels on each breath in and out, the focus of the mind shifts toward feeling and away from thinking and, in turn, the chitter-chatter quietens down.

Bringing your awareness to your breath can be the first step toward building a more present life. My mind used to be full of negative chit-chat. Self-critical thoughts would stop me achieving things I wanted to do, as the downbeat donkey on my shoulder would mutter, "I'm not good enough, I can't do that, I'm not bright enough, confident enough, worthy enough"; each negative thought distracted me from the present moment. It was comforting to realize I wasn't alone. A Harvard study found that humans spend about half of their waking hours thinking about something other than what they're actually doing in that moment. It found that 50 percent of the time participants' minds were wandering from their current reality and that they were significantly less happy when their minds were roaming than when they were focused on the present. This is probably to do with the fact that much of our thinking time can be spent on worries, regrets and replaying the past or fretting over the future. Science has proven that focusing on our breathing can help us regain focus in the present moment.

Due to the close relationship between breath and brain, we can use the breath to retrain the brain and build a deeper sense of self-belief. Negative thoughts may still appear, but will do so less frequently. When they do appear, take a few deep belly breaths, breathing in (belly rises), and notice how the quiet, expansive character of the breath offers you a moment to feel (not think) and creates opportunities to believe in a more positive script. Practising conscious deep breathing can create a space to refocus your mindset. You could view it like tramping though a muddy field, whereby when you are in your headspace, your eyes are fixed downward, and all you can see is thick gooey mud sticking to your boots, your legs are heavy with thoughts and all you can notice in that moment are heavy, muddy, murky thoughts. Yet, going unnoticed, in that same moment all around you is the air, or the "breath space", the sky above you; beyond the rain clouds is a bright blue boundless vista and, within this, the sun shining brightly. If you look up, connect with this breath space, your mind will wander away from sticky, heavy thoughts happening beneath. Consciously switching your attention to another area of your being, from your muddy-field mind to your boundless-sky breath, can help you enter a more expansive, carefree space.

YOU ARE WHAT YOU BREATHE

Every feeling has a unique breathing pattern, which resonates with a particular part of the body. If we are feeling anxious and low, the breath will appear short and shallow in the upper chest. Feelings of love and joy have a free-flowing rhythm, allowing the heart's continual pumping of blood as well as fully expanding the lungs. The magical essence of the breath is that it is both conscious and unconscious. We can tweak our breathing rhythm to change the way we are feeling. If we have learned to breathe a full, healthy breath, we can go from chaos to calm, in less than two minutes. If we are feeling sluggish and sleepy, we can use our breath to pep us up. The breath, like an instrument, can create different rhythms or energy levels and, in turn, allows us to fine-tune the breath to experience new feelings. There's the inhale, the exhale and, in humans, there's also the breath pause.

According to the celebrated and much-loved yogi, the late BKS Iyengar, the breath hold is a natural part of the human respiratory cycle, so much so that it has a name: "kumbhaka", which literally translates as the "retention or holding of the breath, a state where there is no inhalation or exhalation".

Conscious breath-holding during professionally led breathing exercises can benefit the body, so much so that it can increase the endurance of the physiological and the psychological state, and there can be vast improvements in the body and mind.

However, unconscious breath-holding is all too common these days, tied to the meteoric rise in the use of smartphones, and can have an adverse effect on our physiology. Scrolling, texting, swiping are all activities that make us unconsciously hold our breath. I've seen hundreds of clients who after a few breath sessions are suddenly more aware of how they breathe and when they don't breathe. Prolonged breath-holding while using our phones is becoming a modern-day epidemic, so much so that I coined the phrase "tech apnoea", whereby people hold their breath in an unconscious manner while engaged in the unnecessary demands of modern-day technology.

When we unconsciously hold our breath for longer than needed, the body can't function to its optimum; if the body retains the carbon dioxide that it is attempting to expel, subtle and sometimes painful contractions in the diaphragm and intercostal muscles can be experienced, a warning sign to the brain that we must breathe out. During an unconscious breath hold, tension can build up in certain muscles associated with the respiratory system – those of the shoulder, the intercostal muscles and diaphragm. Any extended breath hold indicates to the brain that the body could be in danger and so the body prepares for a "fight or flight" response, which can induce feelings of unease – all the while scrolling through social media.

A full, natural breath is free-flowing and connected, with no pauses between inhalation and exhalation. Such free breathing is pretty hard to find in people; instead we should look to the natural world and to other members of the animal kingdom to learn how to connect ourselves to this graceful flow state of optimal breathing.

" "

WE CAN TWEAK
OUR BREATHING
RHYTHM TO
CHANGE THE WAY
WE ARE FEELING

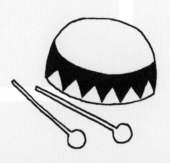

" "

TO SLOW OUR
LIVES DOWN,
IT'S WISE TO
SLOW OUR
BREATH DOWN

BREATHE LIKE A TORTOISE, LIVE LIKE A KING

One of the longest-living animals on earth is the tortoise; the Galapagos tortoise has a lifespan of about 150 years. The tortoise breathes at such a slow rate it is known as the king of breathers. To slow our lives down, it's wise to slow our breath down. During my breath-work training I discovered that my own breath pattern had a quick, shallow pace, which mirrored the way I was living – always wanting to get things done quickly, being impulsive and rushing through life, disconnected from my feelings, apart from the undercurrent feeling of anxiety that made me think I never had enough time to do everything I believed I needed to do in a day. At these times my mind ran like the last sentence, continuously skipping from one thought to the next, without a pause to breathe. I almost feel out of breath remembering this way of living.

Over the years, I've learned to weave conscious breath exercises into my day to manage my energy levels. Such simple tweaks have been life changing. I've managed to slow down both my breathing and my life, I feel more connected to how I feel, more present in the moment, more relaxed, grounded and inspired. More tortoise, less hare.

Despite not being able to enjoy a daily yoga class or regular self-practice these days, as I once did, I do "check in" with my breath throughout the day. Being aware of my breath at these times means I can tap into the way I feel. I follow with a couple of minutes of conscious breathing to help rebalance my mood: I use an energizing breath practice to counter tiredness or a grounding breath exercise to allow me to lose distractions and reconnect with my body. The great thing about conscious breathing is that you can do it anywhere! No need to roll a mat out, light any candles or sit in lotus position. Some of my most effective uses of breath exercises have been while carrying out day-to-day activities, such as queuing, waiting for meetings and commuting, as well as before sleep and on waking. You can weave a breath practice into – and throughout – your day to calm your nervous system and bring peace of mind.

My clients also express that building a closer relationship with their breath pattern and learning to breathe a fuller breath has transformed their lives. One client, Sam, was using an inhaler for ten years before he came across conscious breath work. After a series of sessions he discovered the physical tension he held in his chest was actually an emotional build-up of years of not being able to express how he feels; a familiar pattern in male clients, being brought up in a world where traditionally, to be masculine, there is pressure to be physically strong and the provider. Phrases such as "big boys don't cry", "take it like a man" and "man up" are all too familiar. Emotions are deemed a weakness and are directly associated with being feminine or "girly". Uncontrolled emotions can overwork the nervous system and cause constriction of muscles, such as the smooth muscles of the airways in the lungs. The muscles tense up and constrict, which can worsen wheezing, coughing and tightening of the chest in those living with asthma. Sam is no longer dependent on his inhaler and his attacks have subsided. This coincided with him establishing a regular breath practice, which he says has transformed the way he manages his stress levels. What's more, he feels more comfortable expressing his emotions.

Strong emotions – excitement, fear and anger – can affect the way we breathe. The breath becomes small and constricted. If we arm ourselves with ways to help free tension within the respiratory system in times of stress, we can breathe in a more fluid and relaxed way, which can help calm our nervous system, which in turn sends the message to the brain that we are safe.

Quite simply, learning to breathe fully and consciously has been life-changing, not only for me, but also for those who now use conscious breathing as part of their daily routine. Many answers, it seems, are just under our nose.

GET THE CONSCIOUS-
BREATHING HABIT

Return to calm throughout every day

1 | EYES OPEN
Often, we are told to close our eyes to concentrate on our breathing, but it's more important to become aware of our breathing in the everyday with your eyes wide open.

2 | LYING DOWN
Gently bring your awareness to your body. If you are lying down on your back, make sure you are comfortable. Allow for space between chin and chest to create length in the throat.

3 | OR SITTING
If you are sitting or propped up, allow the spine to be tall and supported. Check for slouching. Uncross the legs. Plant the soles of your feet on the ground. Relax the shoulders. Soften the hands. Release and drop the jaw.

4 | NOTICE
Take your awareness to your breath. Don't change it, simply feel what is happening. Where does the air flow? How does your torso move? Whatever is happening is perfect for now.

5 | COUNTING BREATH
Take a soft, slow inhale through the nose until you come to the end of this sentence. Hold the breath briefly and now exhale fully through the nose, slowly, until you come to the end of this sentence.

5 | REPEAT
Repeat the exercise. Inhale for a count of four. Hold for two. Exhale for six. Continue for up to a minute. Wherever you are, use this exercise throughout your day to bring yourself into the present moment.

CHAPTER 6

STRETCH

STRETCH

A kinder kind of sport

Ruth Williams | Department Store for the Mind
Interviewee: Jackie Field, Ironman athlete, fitness coach and mum

A little powerhouse of joy, enthusiasm and fun whizzes down the path, mud-splattered and rosy cheeked. She is far prettier than her online photos show. Two minutes later I am sat in her kitchen, tea in hand, surrounded by dogs and alone as she and her friend park their off-road bikes and finish their morning training session with a ten-minute run. The view from the back window of her house is breathtakingly beautiful. Trees and green as far as you can see, with no sign of human life visible. A slice of heaven for outdoor lovers and anyone in need of space and fresh air.

Jackie fascinates me. Her list of athletic achievements is impressive, from completing the 2016 Ironman World Championships in Hawaii to achieving a personal best of 3 hours 12 minutes at the 2017 London Marathon. Yet her coaching methods are not concerned with competing and beating others or pushing yourself beyond your limits. I want to know how the suspension of a focus on winning happens alongside this level of success. I also really want to know how she coaches others, what she believes and how she retains all this lightness and enthusiasm under the weight of such physical challenge.

INNER SOULS
Jackie began this athletic chapter relatively recently in her life. Now, with one boy just having started high school and another a few years behind, she is just over a decade into motherhood. I am surprised to learn that the challenges of being a mum were the first chapter of her story. Like so many mums, in the early days she found any time for herself in short supply while knee-deep in all the demands of caring for two boys under five. Conversation with adults was

" "

A DEEPLY SELF-
COMPASSIONATE
APPROACH TO
DISCOVERING AND
DEVELOPING YOUR
PERSONAL BEST
PERFORMANCE

limited to those constantly interrupted chats between mums and dads, which are better than nothing, but don't quite fill that yearning for some sanity-saving adult exchange. You are rarely alone but can be lonely.

Reflecting, Jackie shares that she came to a point where she was probably suffering from postnatal depression. Her youngest son was just over ten months old. She tried to find a group she could join to fit around the childcare, but it was tough. Then she found an early-evening running club and negotiated with her "other half" for a little time off. This first step back to something for herself was a much-needed lifeline out of her depression, a move back to finding out who she was again. She had no idea that it would grow to where it is today.

It started with just running together, enjoying a bit of socializing as Jackie rather than Mum, as well as doing the exercise. Before long, her new running buddies suggested joining the weekend cross-country races. With running-club participation came the occasional question "Would you do a marathon?" At first the idea of the distance seemed daunting. Over time, as she improved, Jackie gave it go and managed to complete one. Then, came the next question: "Would you do a triathlon?" and the reply, "I can't. I can't swim." At this stage Jackie was getting there by just doing. She pushed herself a little further each time, based on confidence gained from her previous success. The conscious awareness of how to develop mental strength came later. Her friends persisted, suggesting joining them for a team triathlon where she could just do one event. This sounded OK, a smaller step, without the need to swim. One borrowed road bike later, she did it again! Another race came up, but this time she would need to do all three events. The swimming training commenced and the journey continued. It was one little step at a time, a gradual process that worked for her. The transition was from initially responding to a new challenge by exploring all the reasons not to do it, to a new way of thinking. The new way was to respond initially by exploring how it could happen, what training would be needed and how to say "yes!" This shift was small but radical.

BEING WITH FRIENDS

As Jackie reflects, she explains that the social side of things was the biggest pull for her in the beginning. She exudes warmth, shows extrovert tendencies and clearly deeply values her friends, by the way she chats about their stories and idiosyncrasies with a wry smile and no hint of negativity. A strong need to fill a social space is no surprise. Finding a way to motivate yourself, driven by an honest understanding of your own strengths, is so helpful. There's a generous amount of acceptance in the way she tells her story and this infectious lively curiosity with the world. It's something of that essence of child-like wonder that we strive to retain as we age. This is interwoven with a serious "no messing" mental strength, creating a combination of soft fluidity and firm determination. I wonder if a little of this rare combination is at the heart of her achievements.

> "FINDING A WAY TO MOTIVATE YOURSELF, DRIVEN BY AN HONEST UNDERSTANDING OF YOUR OWN STRENGTHS, IS SO HELPFUL"

This early chapter in Jackie's story is captured perfectly when she explains that she doesn't really think about training because she just does what she needs to and only does what she enjoys. It is the training she enjoys, the outside time, the social connections. She talks about the process and pleasure of being immersed in the activity, with almost no mention of the outcome. She has shaped her sport her own way and, through the activities, strengthened the power of this individuality.

A COMPETITION REVIVAL?

All sorts of people with various levels of fitness, confidence and motivation join Jackie for off-road riding. She explains that many of them come to her because they just don't feel safe to go out on their own. She opens their eyes to paths already on their doorsteps and demonstrates how to safely navigate a way through. However, it is clearly so much more that she offers people.

"I encourage them to notice how the wheels respond to the ground," explains Jackie, "I vary the rides so the surface changes, from the varying degrees of mud in the winter to something drier in the summer. It's good to get to know the variations." You could describe this as a sort of "active meditation"

where the riders are encouraged to focus on the details of that small area of connection between tyre and ground. While being aware they also need to learn to trust, to feel and adapt rather than to panic and react. Jackie encourages them to slow right down, to create the space to not feel panicked, to not judge themselves harshly. "Learning to feel and adapt will eventually become as natural as walking. But, just like walking, it can feel clumsy as you fall and trip more as you begin to learn. One day something clicks and it takes on an ease, you are in the zone."

Mindfulness in practice is regularly described through examples of focusing on one thing and letting go of any distracting thoughts as they drift into the mind. Jackie explains what happens when riders let go, focus and trust. It sounds very much like they achieve a "flow" state, where we are in the moment, free of judgment and being our optimal selves. The combination of this single focus on the tyre interacting with the ground, alongside Jackie's gentle encouragement to release judgment, brings the rider toward a state of flow.

Jackie's alert to the inner chatter of her group. She retains and retells comments and statements riders share. Often self-critical beliefs. Here is another gem in her approach. She doesn't say, "Don't think about it like that," instead she offers, "Think about it like this..." She shares many examples of how she offers the gentlest, most caring attention to help each of those individuals find their personal, perfectly pitched degree of stretch. As well as shaping this around an understanding of the rider's "inner chatter" she talks about how this can vary, depending on the time of year, the length between rides and the weather. She notices, and she knows. It encourages a deeply self-compassionate approach to discovering and developing your personal best performance through small steps that are pitched at exactly the right point for you. Too far and your confidence may wobble, too easy and there may be no motivating sense of moving forward. It's a simple concept but a fine art. It takes great skills of observation, without judgment, on the part of the coach and is always, when it works well, tailored to the individual.

Falling off is a big part of off-road cycling in the winter months. Parking the ego and setting aside any fears about taking a dive into the mud is one of the best ways to stay in the saddle. New joiners need to learn it's pretty much inevitable.

The sooner they let go of that fear of embarrassment, the easier it becomes. "Falling isn't failing, it's just normal." The more you learn to laugh at yourself and relax, the better. "Winter is a more juvenile time on the bike," explains Jackie, "it's messy and muddy, there will be squeals and laughter. It's fun."

The word "competition" in the original Greek is "*competere*", meaning "to strive with". In this idea, teams or individuals involved in competition are working together to make each other better. Beside one another we create a drive to improve, not by belittling one another, but through motivating one another to discover how far we can personally stretch our potential. Jackie not only coaches the individuals, but facilitates a group dynamic that enables them to do a little of the same for one another.

It sounds as though she flips the mood, so no one needs worry about "keeping up with the rest" because the job of the group is to take care of each other, get there together and only compete as the Ancient Greeks intended.

IT WASN'T THAT BAD...

"Fitness can get you so far but it's mental strength that's the deciding thing," explains Jackie as I attempt to tease out the little nuggets of psychological gold that keep her going for those huge distances with such humility.

So, what does she mean by mental strength and what happens in her head when the body starts resisting?

"It can be hard but you're still listening to your body, you breathe into it and it's that letting go. It's still going to be hard, you accept that it's going to be hard, but hard is not a bad thing. It's just about getting stronger in accepting that.

"Something might be painful when you're first trying to get fit. It's uncomfortable, not pain, and it's just taking you outside of your normal comfort zone. What often happens when we step out of our comfort zone is that we get rigid, but you get through it and realize that it wasn't that bad. This realization of 'it wasn't that bad' gives you the confidence to keep going."

" "

HARD IS NOT
A BAD THING.

IT'S JUST
ABOUT GETTING
STRONGER IN
ACCEPTING THAT

So, she suggests, we begin by finding a different way to think about pain. In doing so, we find another way to feel about stepping outside of our comfort zone. It sounds like we can discover a release from the fear of pain perhaps by realizing we can cope with it. We are stronger than we think.

We explore the connections with yoga (Jackie practises) and the use of the breath to manage restrictions in the body. In many yoga classes you learn to notice and accept the stretch in your muscles, focusing on one area at a time. To not push hard, but to pause with the moment and just breathe into that tense area. There is the meditative role of breath and focus coming into play here too. That simple combination of focus and breath appears to be the way to rethink pain.

The degree of stretch seems crucial to Jackie's mindset. There's something else too. Squashing a fear of failure. I am pretty awe-struck by the example Jackie shares to explain this, though:

"I did a marathon, then people would say, 'Would you ever do an Ironman?' which is the 3.5-mile swim, 112-mile bike and then a marathon, and I thought 'No, that's just ridiculous'. But I did. That's the thing, you do something you thought you couldn't do. You give it a go and risk a fail. But what is a fail? Not completing, is that a fail? Not turning up – to me that's the complete fail. Not giving it a go is failing for me. So, I say 'yes'. That first Ironman made me realize that anyone can train for anything."

BENDING ROUND THE WALL

"Sport means you need to find a way to bend when you hit the challenges." Jackie explains that this could be the potentially big disappointment of having to pull out of an important event due to injury. It could also be the smaller hurdles of just getting up the next muddy peak on a wet day.

When she encounters the challenges, big and small, what happens?

A pause, then a question: "OK, right, so what now?"

In that moment – that pause – she describes accepting that whatever the challenge is has happened. Accepting too that this is not failing, it just is what it is, it's something different rather than right or wrong. She then focuses all her attention and energy on creatively discovering a new way to think about the challenge. A way that will help her find a solution. There is no "beating yourself up". There is no exerting your energy on working out who is to blame, as this will fill you with disappointment. The entire focus is about being here now and looking to find the next small step to move forward.

I think "flexibility" and "agility", but Jackie calls it "bending". And there it is, a simple word for something quite profound! When you hit the challenge, you accept and bend!

"KEEP SLOWING DOWN YOUR THINKING AND SHRINKING THE SIZE OF YOUR TARGET UNTIL THE PANIC SUBSIDES"

I enquire about her personal mantras, trying to discover whether there is a single phrase that Jackie returns to when she needs to bend. There isn't, she explains, "It's about that particular thing, that particular situation." The consistent part of her approach is her mindset, the willingness to bend and the understanding that every single situation is different. It strikes me that it's far simpler, and probably far more powerful, to focus on creating a flexible mindset rather than learning a series of mantras that are likely to be sufficiently varied to respond to the individuality of each challenge.

SLOW AND SMALL
"I don't take in the whole picture. I find whatever is a nice bite-size," Jackie says to explain her personal approach to breaking down the goals that she's working toward during a race.

"Say if it's a race and it's the 112 miles [the bike part of the Ironman], you don't think of it as that far because that sounds like a lot. I think of it as two laps, because two is not a big number. I've just got to do something twice. The first time I am just going to enjoy looking at the scenery, I've never been here and it's beautiful. I ignore the distance. Then one lap is done, and I've only got one lap to go, and that sounds OK."

"Although you're exercising on the bike you're honing in your focus. You have to stay concentrated."

This concept of breaking down the distances into small manageable chunks makes a lot of sense, but I can't help thinking that I'm not sure I could do that. Logically I could work out the numbers, but how do you find that presence of mind to avoid the panic?

"It's about slowing it right down," explains Jackie. "You keep slowing down your thinking and shrinking the size of your target until the panic subsides." This is the point where you are just outside of your own comfort zone. You stay with this and don't even think about pushing it further.

I can't help but wonder how you can do this when surrounded by fellow athletes who may be speeding past as you're slowing down. How do you counteract the self-doubt that comes from feeling unable to keep up with the best?

Jackie barely computes this sort of question because she simply does not care. For her it really is about her personal best and not anyone else's best. For her failing is only "not giving it a go", so if you're there and you're trying then you are succeeding, and she can genuinely let go of the rest.

It strikes me that at the heart of her approach is this idea of not comparing yourself to others. For Jackie, the value of others being there is to share the experience together, not to push others down so you can be the best. So many things in life push us to think we must win or come first. But there is such a tiny minority that can ever achieve this position that it is clearly not a route to the majority finding happiness, satisfaction and a desire to continue taking part. What if we can redefine competition, just as the Ancient Greeks had originally imagined it, to something where the presence of others is thought of as a way to discover our unique and best selves? Then when one person achieves we all do, as we were all part of making that person's success happen. We were there and created the event that meant they could discover their potential.

GET THE KINDER-SPORT HABIT

Ideas for being able to bend

1 | TEMPT YOURSELF

If the exercise itself doesn't tempt you, look for something else about it that draws you in. Perhaps the chance to have some time to yourself or to get a bit of fresh air outdoors?

2 | ONE FOCUS

When you are exercising, find one simple, single thing to focus on, such as the texture of the ground under wheel or foot. Immerse your senses in this one thing.

3 | DISTRACTIONS DRIFT

While focusing on the single thing, other thoughts will appear in the mind. Acknowledge these distracting thoughts and then release them. Let them gently drift away. Bring your focus back to that one simple thing.

4 | PACE

Go slow and don't let the pace of others drive you. Find a pace that makes you feel confident in your abilities. At the right pace, that state of flow can occur when everything just "clicks".

5 | MAKING GOALS WORK

Goals work when they are tailored just for you. Find a level of challenge that is only just outside your comfort zone. Break the distance down until the goal is as small as it can possibly be.

6 | SUBVERT COMPETITION

Think of others, in a race for instance, as people who make it possible for you to discover your personal potential. Remember someone will always be faster and someone will always be slower than you.

CHAPTER 7

TRUST YOUR GUT

TRUST YOUR GUT

The individuality of eating

Meredith Whitely | Food at Heart

There is a particular Monday morning that sticks firmly in my mind.

I'd woken up as normal but, unlike other Monday mornings, my body was struggling to move. And not in the "I can't quite be bothered to get out of bed on a Monday after a big weekend" way. I felt heavy and lethargic, pressed down upon, and my brain was fuzzy. In my woozy state I realized there was no way I could safely drive my long commute to work. It was all I could do to get myself down the stairs and sit huddled on my sofa with a blanket wrapped around me.

It was this morning, and what came after it, that forced me, finally, to face my digestive demons.

I'd initially assumed this affliction was some kind of bug or flu, but a week later it still hadn't quite cleared. I could just about drive, but my body felt out of kilter, and I was oh-so-tired. It was the beginning of a difficult period, which included a conflicted relationship with food. It also marked the start of a slow, gentle journey of, finally, moving toward being more genuinely accepting of my body and its needs.

After lots of medical appointments and tests, it turned out I'm one of the many people in the UK (estimates vary from 10 to 20 percent) who suffer from the set of symptoms grouped together under the term irritable bowel syndrome, or IBS. Of course I was relieved it wasn't something more serious, and believe me when you're sitting through endless screenings there are a hundred concerns running around your brain.

" "

THE SENSORY
PLEASURE OF
SLOW AND MORE
ATTENTIVE EATING
REALLY PAID OFF
AS IT ALLOWED
ME TO ENJOY
FOODS IN A
DIFFERENT WAY

However, the problem with IBS is that it's a highly individual condition and there's no such a thing as a cure, though food is a big part of it.

What isn't always spoken about in relation to this condition is the need for emotional healing. Being told you "just" have IBS doesn't take into account the tears from stomach pain that wake you in the middle of the night. Or the embarrassment of standing in front of the mirror with a protruding belly that looks three months pregnant and won't fit into jeans that were perfectly comfortable yesterday. Or the fear of eating out, in case you need to rush to the toilet, or else sit with stabbing aches during what is supposed to be a fun, social occasion.

A particular challenge for me was that I defined a big part of myself through my love of creating and eating good food. I cared about food, where it came from and the people who grew and made it. I cooked a lot, ate mostly organic, a lot of plant-based food and was doing many things around diet and exercise that were, on the face of it, very right. But my body and, in particular, my stomach and gut were telling me that something was wrong.

The truth is that that Monday was a culmination of many years of only partially listening to my body. This was not just in relation to what I was eating, but also how I was managing my stress and, the big surprise to me, my self-compassion. What I now recognize as a digestive flare-up didn't come out of nowhere.

TAPPING INTO DIGESTIVE STRESSES

I had suffered from a "sensitive digestion" for as long as I could remember. When I was stressed or overworked, my gut was one of the first things that started to complain, so much so I got used to it and just carried on regardless. Even when I picked up the dreaded parasite *Giardia lamblia* while in Peru, and all its unpleasant side effects, I hadn't noticed; the doctor seemed more than a little surprised I hadn't come in sooner to get checked out.

In addition, like so many people, I had, and have, a sometimes complicated relationship with food and my body. I loved food wholeheartedly: cooking, eating and reading about food filled much of my spare time. But I allowed myself to be frightened by it, too. I had some unhealthy ways of thinking about food, even though at the same time it was such a passion.

Now knowing about my IBS, I was scared of how some foods might make me feel physically. But there was a more insidious fear sneaking in underneath that I might overeat or eat "bad" foods and gain weight. This anxiety was exacerbated by trying to judge good and bad foods in relation to my digestive symptoms.

While I didn't have an eating disorder, I definitely had some disordered approaches to food. I'd never bought into prescribed diets as such, as most of them appeared, even to the untrained eye, to be a load of old codswallop (as well as not very tasty). But I had restricted my food intake at times and been overly interested in the nutritional side of food instead of just enjoying the good variety of foods I was already eating.

For many years I, too, was sucked into thinking low-fat was the way forward. I grew up at the tail end of the Seventies and into the Eighties; the acknowledged "wisdom" was that fat was bad, margarine was healthier than butter and being meat-free was mainly for hippies. Though, as a slight hippy-at-heart, the last did resonate with me.

Without realizing it, I had also developed some rather rigid rules around what constituted a healthy diet, even though no one would have known, as these rules encompassed quite a lot of food. This meant eating whole and organic foods and avoiding treat foods, processed foods and too many carbs. These invisible rules also had me perusing menus in great detail, often before I visited somewhere, to make sure I always chose the healthiest option, rather than listening to what I really wanted. Although the healthy option was often what I genuinely wanted, as I knew it made my body feel good or sounded delicious, honestly this wasn't always the reason I made my meal choices. I also continued to eat some foods, such as chickpeas and lentils, because they were deemed healthy – even though my gut was telling me it really didn't enjoy them in the same way my tastebuds did.

Stress is a common trigger for IBS and, rather unhelpfully, trying to manage my situation and my eating was stressing me out. I wanted to fight this

condition, heal myself, make things better and just be able to enjoy what I was eating without worrying. If I'm honest, I did feel a bit hard done by, when I looked at what other people were eating without any problems.

The big surprise for me was that fighting wasn't the best solution.

There were a few things about how food made me feel that I needed to unpick, but going into battle against this was not the solution. It was much more about accepting and being compassionate with my body, learning not to demonize food and to think about my life and body in its totality. It was instead a slow and gentle process of compassionate learning about what foods and habits worked best for my body. This included a general slowing down and letting go a little of some of the restrictive rules I'd unintentionally been applying in my life (though I do still kinda miss having chickpeas in my life – see, I told you I was a bit of a hippy).

THE POWER OF SIMPLE AND SLOW

So much of the way we think about food focuses on *what* we eat. Of course this is important, but I would argue that *how* we eat – and how we live – should form part of the discussion when it comes to eating well, in a compassionate way and in a way that is enlivening.

An interesting side effect of my digestive problems was that I started to eat much more slowly and mindfully. At the time I hadn't even realized this is one of the approaches recommended for managing digestive issues.

It happened almost unintentionally through my struggles to eat, as I'd naturally slowed down, but also through the preceding years of my growing dedication to dark chocolate. To taste chocolate properly you have to taste it slowly, using all your senses. Working with chocolate is also an incredibly mindful experience as you have to give it your full attention. Little did I know that chocolate – of all foods – would be one of the teaching and healing tools that would help me move back to a much happier place with food. I often now describe chocolate as a gateway food to experiencing the pleasure of slower, more mindful eating.

Eating in this way also made me notice that many of the rituals around food that naturally slow us down, including traditional ways we connect with others through food, are on the wane. In our busy lives, meals are packed in around everything else and time together at the table also gets squeezed.

"IT WAS A SLOW AND GENTLE PROCESS OF COMPASSIONATE LEARNING ABOUT WHAT FOODS AND HABITS WORKED BEST FOR MY BODY"

Let me give you an example from my childhood. Although I'm no longer a practising Catholic, I was brought up in the faith. Before all meals, even at school, we would pause to say grace, which included an appreciation of, and gratitude for, the food we were about to eat and the hands that made it. We also had a family tradition on Sundays after church of sitting around the table for long, leisurely *mezze*-style meals in which we talked, ate and enjoyed being together. I have such fond memories of the food, conversations and celebrations of that time.

I no longer say grace and, with most of my family living in Australia, while I live in the UK, I don't often have the chance to relive these big group meals. But I do have a few of my own pause rituals. I try to remember to take a few breaths before eating rather than diving straight in. I take small mouthfuls and finish them before rushing on to the next one. I always thank another person who has prepared a meal for me, normally my husband. And I treasure the times of eating with other people.

CALM MIND, HAPPY GUT

This healing power of slowing down didn't just apply to my eating.

What I hadn't recognized was that for many years I'd been living in a fairly consistent state of low-level anxiety. I am a happy and enthusiastic person, but that natural energy and caring can manifest in a negative way, in the form of perfectionism and overly harsh self-criticism. It was also perhaps where some of my "food rules" had originated.

The internal tussle with my perfectionism, and the little voice telling me success only comes through working harder and harder, was speaking through my gut.

Small, relatively unimportant things would loom large in my mind, particularly if I'd made a mistake at work or thought I might have unintentionally upset someone. Thoughts about this kept me awake at night or ran around my brain throughout the day. They sometimes even stopped me truly enjoying time off or being fully present with people I cared about. But my solution to managing this, weirdly, was to do more, try and be more, work harder still.

Our emotions, mental health and stress are intrinsically linked with our gut. Feeling stressed was not helping my digestive system, even if I was eating well.

And it seems that in the scientific world, this connection between mind and gut goes both ways, according to a study in 2014 (see page 154). You probably already know the power of gut feelings first-hand from those butterfly sensations when you get nervous or excited. The gut sends signals to your brain via the network of millions of nerve cells embedded in its walls that control the reflexes of the gastrointestinal system. In addition, the gut is responsible for producing up to 90 percent of the mood-regulating neurotransmitter serotonin. And then there's the general health of our gut microbiome – the population of bacteria that live within us – that is implicated in all sorts of areas of our lives. Our guts therefore have a pivotal role in helping us feel good. So, when your gut's not in a good state, it's hard for the rest of you to be happy.

I needed to extend the slowness, the gentleness, to my sensitive gut – and myself. This gentleness included going back to basics and, for a period, focusing on super-simple foods, building up to a big enough variety that my gut could handle.

So often we are tempted by the buffet of life and all we could, or feel we should, be doing or eating. It seems there is a huge fear of missing out, so we end up piling a load of different things on to our plates.

I used to do this, quite literally, during my lunch breaks at one of my favourite salad-bar haunts when I first worked in London. It had an amazing mix of hot- and cold-filled silver trays, brimming with lunch possibilities, laid out to be scooped up with wild abandon into takeaway boxes. And, of course, you'd try to get as much into the box as possible, especially being on a tight first-job budget. But it was kind of overwhelming for my gut, and in the end everything mixed together so, disappointingly, I couldn't really taste the different parts.

Needless to say, this is not how I approach buffets, or indeed life, now. Today, I have a better sense of what is "just enough" for me. And eating more mindfully has been a big part of this, with lots of trial and error along the way.

At first, eating mindfully can feel a bit clunky, as you place the effort of your attention on your different senses, chewing slowly and putting your cutlery down between mouthfuls. But you soon start to appreciate the beauty of repetition and recognition of the new in foods you've eaten a million times before, whether it be a cup of tea sipped in silence or a piece of chocolate nibbled in concentration.

The sensory pleasure of slow and more attentive eating really paid off as it allowed me to enjoy foods in a different way, rather than being scared of them. I could suspend self-judgment and fear, even if just for a few moments at times, as I was so focused on the act of taste. It has also meant, longer term, being more compassionate with myself about my food choices and allowing myself to enjoy foods I'd previously classified as off limits for health or digestive reasons.

Reconnecting with the simple, taking pleasure in the slow and noticing the small details have all been important parts of my healing.

SELF-COMPASSION AND LOVING KINDNESS

As you can probably tell, getting back to a happier place of food appreciation was about much more than what was on my plate. So much information exists on the "shoulds" and "shouldn'ts" of eating well. Layer on food-related health problems and all the other "shoulds" we carry around in our lives and it can feel, well, overwhelming.

One of the other major areas I've needed, and continue, to work on is being more compassionate with myself and recognizing unhelpful "shoulds".

My natural instinct was to make myself better, to make up for what I thought was the lack in my body that meant it was broken. But this fighting only made me tense, jarring against my body. Again, slowly, initially supported by cognitive behavioural therapy (CBT) sessions, more reading and lots of rest, I came to realize the importance of daily habits of self-care and self-compassion.

It was incremental and gentle experiments around what food, behaviours and practices worked for me that ended up making the big difference. It's probably no huge surprise to know that meditation – something else that used to be seen as the province of hippies –was also significant. In fact, its positive impact led me to train as a meditation teacher.

I've turned to one particular meditation, focusing specifically on self-compassion, many times. Originally from the Buddhist tradition, and now incorporated in secular mindfulness practice, it is called "loving kindness" or "metta" meditation.

The traditional meditation moves through a repetition of a compassionate phrase, which is something like:

"May I be happy. May I be well. May I be safe. May I be peaceful and at ease."

It is repeated again, bringing various people to mind, before being extended to the wider world. It is a very calming meditation in and of itself, but in the last decade a number of small-scale studies indicated that compassion meditation can help counter self-criticism and, astoundingly, even lower levels of inflammation in the body. Through gentle repetition of such a phrase, we can reframe our thinking, our feeling, our reactions, including those toward ourselves.

When I look back now over the years of regular, now daily, practice, I recognize the changes in the way I speak to myself, including when it comes to making food choices and when I start to get frustrated with my body. And, to be clear, this is not about running away from emotions or sugar-coating them, as I was sometimes doing before. Meditation has been a powerful tool in allowing me to experience these feelings and to spot – and catch myself – if I return to old patterns of self-criticism or rigid food rules.

Don't get me wrong, I'm not saying meditation will suddenly make you love your body or eat only food that makes you feel good. But for me it has been another tool to help me recognize when I'm not being kind to myself and has given me a framework for using more positive language and reactions that extend far beyond my formal practice.

I want to be totally upfront here.

I'm not cured.

I don't have a sexy diet or solution that you can put a name on and package up with a clear list of "dos and don'ts".

I haven't become a whole new person. I am still me, but more like the real me, if that doesn't sound too cheesy.

I'm much better at managing my symptoms when they do flare up. I even have a strange gratitude for the difficult journey my dodgy digestion has taken me on, as it had led to a much greater understanding of myself.

And – a big one – I'm also better at accepting my body as it is now, and even how it might be in the future, with all its strengths and limitations. Even though I still feel upset at times, I don't feel the need to run away, or to fight, but instead to try to treat myself as I would a good friend, with compassion and care.

I still have a long way to go, but I'm now mostly excited rather than scared about where this tasty and enlightening journey will take me.

GET THE SLOW-EATING HABIT

Ideas for developing slow-eating rituals

1 | ONE PRACTICE
Think of one practice you could adopt at your next meal to slow yourself down.

2 | ONE BREATH
You might: take one breath before you eat.

3 | ONE MOUTHFUL
Or, eat just one mouthful at a time.

4 | NOTICE COLOUR
Or, notice the colours on your plate.

5 | JUST ENOUGH
And consider this – what does "just enough" look like and feel like to you?

6 | NOTICE CHANGE
Notice how this one practice affects your eating experience. How does your body feel? What happens to your mind and emotions while you eat? How do you feel in body, mind and mood immediately after eating? Then check in again an hour or two later.

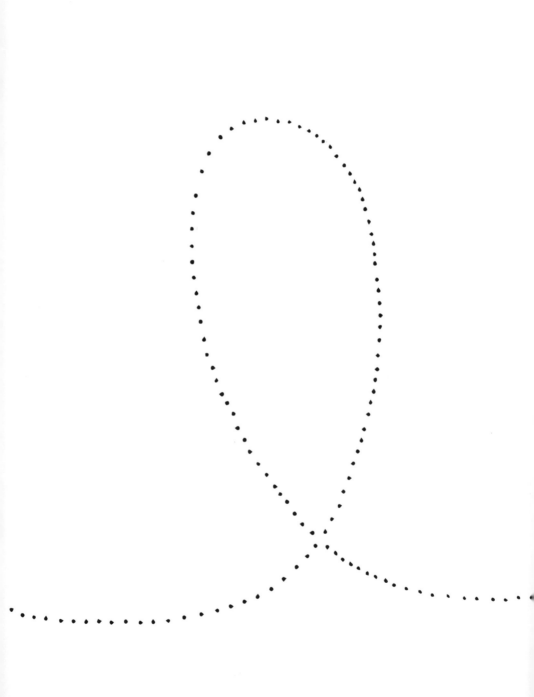

CHAPTER 8

MY WAY

MY WAY

Choosing life with the good stuff in mind

Gemma Brady | Sister Stories

Life changed the day I opened the tin of black paint.

I was sitting on my living-room floor, having dashed out to the shops to buy a vat of a bold, beautiful, dark colour to adorn my walls. Stirring the pot in preparation, I felt the thrill of the unexpected. This spontaneous purchase was highly uncharacteristic. Usually, a project as grave as decorating a room would have required months of planning in meticulous detail and painting dozens of colour samples upon the wall to conduct a forensic analysis of how each hue would look in different light.

But that day, the flash of an idea came to me, and by the evening, I had a black living room. It looked glorious and wild and stylish. I felt giddy with boldness.

That day marked a significant internal shift. Life had somehow moved from being a dutiful march of progression toward a set of societal expectations and personal goals, to a vast canvas on which to experiment. It had been so simple: I'd had a fun idea and acted upon it immediately, trusting the creative spark. I started to realize that when we begin to recognize the creative potential that we all possess, life opens up in the most glorious ways. We can move from having a "paint by numbers" life to taking our tools and carving out a way of living that works for us, using the individual gifts we have been given.

IN NOTHING THERE IS EVERYTHING

I had spent years working in the creative industries, exhausted by the pressure to craft exceptional work to a deadline. I felt I had been running on

" "

WHAT WOULD LIFE
LOOK LIKE IF WE
ALL CONSIDERED
OURSELVES ARTISTS,
ARCHITECTS AND
SCULPTORS WHO
ARE CARVING OUT
OUR INDIVIDUAL
EXISTENCE, MOMENT
BY MOMENT?

a never-ending treadmill – produce, deliver, produce, deliver – for many years, and the stuffing had been knocked out of me. This fatigue, combined with unexpected major surgery, meant it was time to stop. It was clear the only way to proceed was to take time out to lick my wounds and attend to my health.

At around the same time, the flat I'd shared for years had become my own. I wanted to mark my first experience of home ownership with some changes to the space. A pot plant here, a new mirror there, perhaps even a fresh set of curtains: my ambition was limited. I was tired. The project felt a chore, and my spirit sank at the idea of trips to hardware stores. I did nothing. I committed myself, for the first time in my life, to rest.

In a culture that values the endless pursuit of productivity, there is little time for true idleness. Hours are spent scrolling through social media, days pass in a blur of boxsets, but moments of true rest are often strictly confined to sleep. The media often reminds us that the blue light of screens messes with the melatonin in our brain, negatively affecting our sleep, and that the reward-loop of social media stimulates the production of dopamine and feeds us a consequent high. Nevertheless, I had ignored this advice, assuming that consuming more information and more content fuelled a creative brain. It was just a different way of learning, wasn't it? I later discovered it was having quite the opposite effect, draining me of energy and the ability to think in new ways.

During my enforced period of rest, I deleted social-media apps from my phone, laid down my reading list and languished in bed, watching the changing light cast beautiful shapes on the wall. I'd occasionally slip on my shoes for a shuffle round the local park, where I forgot my bursting podcast subscription list and listened to the birds and rustle of leaves. The water of the lake glinted at me, requiring nothing in return.

Life was lived as a moving meditation.

The thought of being still had once terrified me and yet, in these months, the art of being idle became a source of joy and relief. I savoured this new way of living, with only the occasional pang of longing for the adrenaline kick of my previous existence.

With each week that passed in a gentle blur of nothingness, I was able to surrender into rest more. I passed the days reading, pottering, napping and having no expectations of myself. I had never known such an unstructured way of living. No deadlines, no obligations, just the radically simple act of being. It was like being born afresh.

Learning to simply be is one of the greatest challenges of modern life, but one of the greatest gifts when we find it.

Little by little, I could feel something awakening inside myself. A gently simmering creativity at play. Having put down the bag of rocks I'd been carrying, unsurprisingly life felt lighter and my inclination to dance, rather than plod, grew. I noticed the small joys of life again: the sensation of the water falling upon my head in the shower, the warm breeze that promised summer and the simplicity of letting each day unfold at its own pace.

Slowly, my energy started to return.

But more than that: my mind began to fill with inspiration. I found that in cultivating space for nothing, an abundance of energy and ideas started to flourish. I'd had a meditation practice for years, but it was always squeezed into an over-packed diary, taken as a snatched moment of quiet, the allocated ten minutes mostly being occupied with squishing thoughts from the "to do" list. Not quite the Zen master approach to meditation...

What started to become clear to me was that learning to cultivate a quiet mind was not about adding it to the day's never-ending list of tasks, but rather committing to finding space, however hectic life was. It felt that in order to find more joy in life, I had to do less. A curious realization for an over-achiever, but a valuable one.

THE ROAD WELL TRAVELLED

Let's go back to the beginning. Since I was very small, I wanted to achieve things. I recall toddling up to my teacher, requesting a delightful after-school activity I'd heard the older children discuss: "homework". I was horrified when

this terribly serious and carefully considered request was met with a tinkle of laughter and "There's plenty of time for homework when you're older." Did my teacher not realize that in order to live a good and productive life, one had to fiercely commit to working consistently and hard? Especially when one was six years old. I was sure that it was a particularly important time to lay strong foundations.

"IN CULTIVATING SPACE FOR NOTHING, AN ABUNDANCE OF ENERGY AND IDEAS STARTED TO FLOURISH"

The route to success, it felt, was laid out before me. Years of diligent and excessive work at school would lead to excellent exam results, a place at a top university and then I would be "safe". There was a well-trodden path to be walked, and I was determined to lace up my boots and dedicate myself to the journey with the commitment of a soldier heading out to the battlefield. If there was a sufficient amount of jaw-clenching and effort involved, all would be well, surely? What a relief.

As the world of work beckoned, I found myself drawn to a career in television. This was a shock, as despite my love for the arts, I'd always imagined I'd end up in a profession with defined boundaries, such as a lawyer. Where there was one way to do things, and a right or wrong answer. I'd decided, in the interests of safety, that I wasn't a creative person. That I wanted to follow in the footsteps of others rather than forge my own path. But the world of making programmes held a seductive sheen, and I was soon a thriving television producer.

The electric energy of working was enthralling. As my confidence grew, I committed myself to storytelling. I loved the art of developing relationships with people in order to help them voice their experiences and it played to my strengths. I found myself frequently experiencing the state of "flow" which Dr Mihaly Csikszentmihalyi and the positive psychology movement have identified as key to human happiness. When we are in this state, we are so deeply involved in creating that all sense of time is lost.

Flow sounds just marvellous, doesn't it? But can a person experience too much flow? I'd argue that you can.

In pursuit of great work, the human spirit can flourish, but it can also be eroded. For me, the pressure and pace of the jobs I was doing wore down my body and mind. My frazzled adrenal glands worked overtime, masquerading as being "in the zone". My creative impulses had long left me, and it was all I could do to put one foot in front of the other on a path that did not feel my own.

Having the brakes slammed on was a turning point and the best lesson in creativity I could have received.

EUDAEMONIA – THE GOOD LIFE

The Ancient Greeks, led by Aristotle, encouraged the pursuit of "eudaemonia" – living the good life. Martin Seligman, the father of the positive psychology movement, drew on Aristotle's teachings when he laid out his theory of how to achieve authentic happiness. To paraphrase Seligman, when Aristotle spoke of eudaemonia he was not concerned with the hedonistic thrill of parties or shopping or receiving 100 likes on Facebook, but rather with the simple pleasures of contemplation and the enjoyment of being engaged in meaningful activity. This was the predecessor of Dr Mihaly's flow state.

In studying the pursuit of happiness, many great minds have agreed on one thing: a life well lived is one of simple pleasures.

In the months when I was resting and started to feel myself come alive again, I recalled reading another interpretation of this ancient concept. Writer Liz Gilbert's *Big Magic* is a charming exploration of what it means to live a creative life, and links eudaemonia and the creative muse: "In Greek, the word for the highest degree of human happiness is eudaemonia, which basically means 'well-daemoned.' The Greeks and Romans believed in a daemon of creativity... who sometimes aided you in your labours. Your genius – your guardian deity, the conduit of your inspiration."

This idea of creativity as a helpful daemon made me consider again where our creative impulses come from. In my months of slowing down, I realized that through my pushing and striving and scrolling, I'd been stomping all over my creative daemon. It had been working 16-hour days six days a week and had never been given the opportunity to pop over to a beach resort for some time on a sun-lounger.

"I BEGAN TO PLAY WITH THE IDEA THAT LIFE DIDN'T HAVE TO BE SO HARD"

In rest, I came to believe that there really is a "daemon" inside us, a part of the human spirit that needs treating gently and respectfully in order to flourish. When I was rested, I started to notice that ideas were coming to me freely and frequently, in unexpected forms. Quite unexpected. One day I had a very detailed idea for an app to help people with the flu who live alone and need help, another day one came to me for a business involving printer cartridges and, another, the plot of a novel. I acted upon none of these (my knowledge of printer cartridges is cursory at best), but enjoyed the fact my brain was working in new ways. I learned that from silence and idleness comes great creative potential.

But, much more importantly, I began to play with the idea that life didn't have to be so hard.

LIVING LIFE MY WAY

Having been in hibernation and not yet ready to restart work just yet, the flat renovation felt like a nice bridge back to normal living. I experienced sparks of excitement at the possibility once more.

There was no scanning of home magazines and blogs to see how other people had done things, no searching for what was on trend. It felt liberating to just sit and wait until an idea of what I wanted my home to look like struck me.

119

In the moment I splashed black paint over the walls of my living room, I decided this: living is itself a creative act. Each of us has an individual tapestry to weave with intention and joy, and there need be no pattern to follow. Having been a rules-follower and equation-balancer for so long, it felt wild to whisper: "maybe there is another way".

"CREATIVE LIVING IS TURNING OUR ATTENTIONS TOWARD WHAT ENERGIZES US"

We follow the path laid out before us, dictated by the industries we work in, the societies we live in and the expectations that are placed upon us. What would life look like if we all considered ourselves artists, architects and sculptors who are carving out our individual existence, moment by moment?

Life begins to open up when we realize our potency, when our grip on the rules loosens and when we can dance with the daemons a bit more.

I started to experiment with living my life as if I were an artist considering her next piece of work. What do I want it to convey? What would I like it to look like? What materials will I use? Which influences do I want to incorporate in my masterpiece?

LIFE IS EASY FOR ME, NOW

When I was finding life particularly challenging a few months before I had to stop working, my friend and teacher Gail Schock once suggested that I repeat the phrase "Life is easy for me", until I believed it. At the time, I was about to run the New York Marathon. I'd run several marathons before (see, over-achieving personality type) and was worried that my training wouldn't see me get a new personal best. Anxiety-ridden, I decided to try something dangerous and new. I left my watch at home. Rather than checking my speed and watching the miles crawl by in excruciating 0.1-mile increments, I felt my heart soar with the pleasure of running through the five boroughs of this magical city in autumn. As any marathon runner knows, 26.2 miles can feel, well, rather a long way. It flew by. It truly did. And when I tumbled over the finish line, my time was only a few minutes slower than it would had been if I'd been putting myself through the excruciating process of furious clock-watching. The experience could have been very difficult, or it could have been easy. I chose easy.

WORKING WITH WHAT YOU HAVE

Armed with easeful experiences such as this and my new artistic approach to creating my own future, I decided to make a list of all the qualities that came naturally to me and that I enjoyed using the most. I asked myself: How could I maximize the time I spent using these gifts? Did you flinch when I said the word "gifts"? Many of us do. But we all possess a unique set of qualities that, if we can find ways to work and play with them, can enable us to live a beautiful, easy (OK, easier) life.

The criteria for making decisions changed. Success felt less important. I forgot the "input equals output" equation I'd lived by up until then.

This commitment to a new way of being involved a fair bit of moving around of my internal furniture, scraping it along the walls as I went. It was challenging to accept the idea that fiercely pursuing a meteoric rise to the top of the television industry was not going to help me live a happy, creative life. Six-year-old me and her lofty aspirations was pretty furious at that one; she still wants more homework. There was also a period of grieving for the life I thought I was going to have, which I knew had to let go of. Once the upset had been experienced fully, a new sense of possibility bubbled up inside. Life could truly be the varied tapestry I'd dared to dream of.

I realized that the empathy and listening skills that had served me well in telling sensitive stories in the world of TV could serve others. I trained as a life coach and developed a particular interest in how creating quiet, expectation-free spaces can help people discover their own potential afresh. I now help women work through personal and creative challenges they're experiencing in their lives, finding a deep sense of pleasure in the conversations I engage in. I started a movement – called Sister Stories – to bring women together to enjoy the community and connection that can arise out of telling our own stories. This almost didn't happen, as I didn't want the pressure of finding an event space, but as I sat in my cosy black living room, I realized there was no better place to start than here. Life is easy for me.

I still make television programmes, but have to feel my inner creative daemon leap with joy at the prospect of the project. At my core, I'm someone who helps stories come into the world, be it helping individuals make sense of their own, writing them or helping them come to life on film. When I started to realize that doing this not only didn't require me to run myself into the ground, but also gave me lots of space and rest, life started to feel really quite exciting again.

Creative living is turning our attentions toward what energizes us. It really is that simple.

When we start to see ourselves as artists experimenting in the world, the potential of what we can do explodes. We each have, moment to moment, the power to create things that didn't exist hours before. It could be a black wall, a new way of using up the leftovers in the fridge or a wholesale lifestyle change – whatever makes us enjoy life a little more. Through slowing down, allowing our overcrowded brains rest and enjoying the "nothingness", we can charge our creative and emotional batteries. Start to do things our way. Choose to step away from being shaped by expectation and let the act of living become an art form.

GET THE CREATIVE HABIT

Ideas for waking up your creativity

1 | DO-NOTHING TIMER

Sit – set a timer for ten minutes and sit quietly, free of distractions. If you can, make it a daily habit. The more space you give your brain, the more space there is for new ways of thinking to arise.

2 | PLAY

Do something uncharacteristic or unexpected just for fun. Surprise yourself.

3 | LIFE ART

Consider life a work of art. Faced with a task or situation you don't like? Consider how your creative power could help you do things another way.

4 | NOTICE YOU

Notice what happens to your inner chatter, emotions and physical sensations when you inject creativity into problem-solving in life.

5 | NOTICE OTHERS

Notice what happens to the behaviour of people around you when you throw away the rule book and problem-solve together more creatively. Perhaps reflect together on what happens, if it feels right to do this.

6 | MAKE IT STICK

When any of these ideas work, take a little time to reflect. Maybe record the experience in your journal, if you have one. Then think about, or simply look out for, the next opportunity to put the approach into action again. Keep this cycle going. Before you know it, creativity will be popping up throughout your day.

CHAPTER 9

LAUGHTER LINES

LAUGHTER LINES

A celebration of the passage of time

Gemma Brady | Sister Stories

I was born with big ears.

It was, in many ways, appropriate, as over the years I've learned that the role I play in life is as a listener.

It is through listening to others that, from the very earliest age, we shape our world view. We learn what it is to be human by absorbing the experiences of those who have gone before. Wisdom passes between generations.

Being big-eared and curious was fun. Long before I told stories for a living, I listened out for them; thirsty for tales that would help me understand more about this higgledy-piggledy world I lived in. All I knew was that I didn't know much. And that there were wise people out there who could help me.

Over the years, I have sought the wisdom of elders time and time again. I slowly started to realize that every time they told me a story, they were whispering wisdom to their younger selves. The lessons they'd wished they'd grasped sooner and were hoping I'd grasp now.

The word "elder" has a simple definition – someone who is older than you. But it also has a meaning more heavy with history: "a leader or senior figure in a tribe or other group". And the Hebrew word for "elder" literally means "beard", a term packed with connotations of wisdom. All very serious. Over time, I've come to associate conversations with elders as an opportunity for fun – I've rarely encountered a terribly serious "beard".

" "

GROWING
OLDER NEED
NOT BE AN
EXPERIENCE
OF LOSS, BUT
A GENTLE
HARVESTING OF
EXPERIENCES
OVER TIME,
WHICH LIVE
ON IN THE
CORNERS
OF OUR MIND

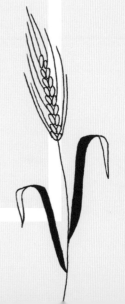

Growing older can mean gathering a collection of lived stories or fables. Listening to the tales of elders can act as a manual for living, not necessarily in action but in spirit. If we experienced life's ups and downs as chapters of one great story, how might that change our experience of living?

Each story here is a gift from an elder, a lesson from those who have lived a full life and learned how both self-acceptance and acceptance of the ups and downs of being human is the key to a happy, fulfilled existence.

THE TINY APPRENTICE: LESSONS IN LISTENING

The power of learning to be grateful has been known for centuries and has grown to be an expanding area of psychological research. Since Robert Emmons' inaugural work into the power of gratitude in 2007, multiple studies have shown that gratitude improves mental and physical wellbeing, improving everything from self-esteem and sleep to cortisol levels and blood pressure.

My earliest memory of learning to be grateful started when I was dispatched to the house of an elderly lady called Margaret to help her polish her brass ornaments. I was a Brownie (girl scout) and this was one of the tasks given to me to earn a crucial badge. My mum dropped me at the door and it felt terribly exciting to walk into a stranger's house and discover what treasures lay inside. Perhaps, like my own grandparents, she'd have something sweet waiting for me or, even better, a *Wizard of Oz* video to watch.

I was ushered into a room groaning with old oak furniture, and instructed to clamber up onto a large chair. There were a series of brass candlesticks and trinkets laid out before me, with two cloths. As I was instructed to carefully use the polish to buff the surface, Margaret told me about how her husband had died last year, and how nice it was to have company to polish the brass. At age nine, I was at a loss at how to respond appropriately to this news of a death, so I sat and buffed my candlestick and just listened. She told me how, every month in retirement, they'd sit down on a Tuesday afternoon, take out the polish and lose themselves in the slow pleasure of making the candlesticks and ornaments shine again. As she talked of her late husband, her eyes crinkled so beautifully and her face was glowing with happiness. I remember puzzling about how she could be so happy that her husband was dead. Later, I recalled this afternoon and realized that in the act of polishing, she was enjoying the times she'd shared with her late husband, turning them over in her mind and letting the memories delight her afresh.

Our experiences, when treasured, become memories that bring pleasure again and again. Growing older need not be an experience of loss, but a gentle harvesting of experiences over time, which live on in the corners of our mind. Margaret was taking out a precious recollection of her husband and polishing it gently, so when she held it up to the light and shared it with a stranger, it glimmered. Her gratitude was visible and overshadowed any sense of loss.

"SO OFTEN, THE EXTRAORDINARY LAY IN THE ORDINARY"

It wasn't all misty-eyed reminiscing in Margaret's house. There was work to be done. After the brass polishing had been completed, I was dispatched into the kitchen to fetch her handbag. My mind once again turned to sweet things or the promise of a coin. Alas, no such luck. We were going to clean out her handbag with a vacuum cleaner. I'd never heard of such a thing. Such cleaning was for carpets and getting cobwebs out of corners, not for leather goods, surely.

Little by little, Margaret emptied out its contents onto the dining-room table, setting them into a neat line. A lipstick, a pack of tissues, a brass comb (I prayed she wouldn't make me polish it) and some errant coins that had escaped her purse. She handed me a cloth and encouraged me to buff away any dust and dirt on the items. She told me it was important in life to be grateful for what we have and always to take care of the things we are so lucky to own.

In a world of quick-fix fashion, it's easier to purchase a new handbag online than it is to poke one's head into the recesses of the old one. Today, a cleaner can be dispatched to your home with the push of a button on an app. But long

before the comfort-blanket of the smartphone, Margaret had cultivated a set of habits that soothed her soul and made her eyes sparkle as she enjoyed the simple pleasure of keeping the things she owned spick and span. For Margaret, these acts were born of pride and thankfulness, and whatever was happening in the outside world, she'd return to polishing those candlesticks or clearning out that handbag.

The simple value of ritual

I grew up to be a documentary maker, a line of work that has led me to sit listening to many life stories. In her book *Do Story: How to tell your story so the world listens* Bobette Buster talks about seeking out "the gleaming detail" of a story – "the one thing that captures both the emotion and idea of the story at once".

In my conversations with people I wanted to film, I'd start, magpie-like, to dig around for the gleaming detail of a situation or relationship that would help crystallize an important element of the tale.

Working in a team of talented storytellers taught me that so often, the extraordinary lay in the ordinary. I learned to ask questions that allowed the ordinary to take centre stage. It felt funny to be asking people to recount in such forensic detail the outfit they were wearing when they met their husband or what their favourite meal was, but this seeking out of the gleaming detail was to reveal great lessons that I've carried with me ever since.

A common theme that my older interviewees would often return to were the simple but meaningful rituals that had shaped their lives.

I recall once listening to an interview with a delightful British man named John, who told the story of how, 70 years earlier, he'd seen a "shapely piece" walk into the room and decided this was his wife-to-be. The man sitting in front of the camera was 90 and to hear him describe the woman he fell in love with in this way felt nothing less than gloriously charming.

He recalled their first date: 28 June 1946. As he talked to camera, he told tales of their blossoming romance and the rituals they developed. In their courting days, he'd take her to the movies and together they created shared rituals: "We'd have beans on toast afterwards and if I had an extra sixpence, we'd have chips as well!"

The foundations of a long marriage were laid by co-creating simple, shared rituals. These experiences bonded the young lovers and over time became a symbolic touchstone to enjoy together, no matter what uncertainties the world was throwing at them.

John continued… "The first film we saw was *The Dark Corner*. It was shown on television many years later, and I taped it. So when we have special celebrations, we have beans on toast and we watch the film."

"SIMPLE PLEASURES MIGHT BE EXACTLY WHAT WE NEED"

Now in her eighties, his wife has Alzheimer's disease, and the tender moments shared are fewer and further between. But some constants remain: the pleasure of popping two slices of bread in the toaster, opening a can of Heinz and settling into a familiar habit that, despite 70 years having passed, remains unchanged.

The word "ritual", once heavy with connotation of religion or solemnity, has a new place in our modern world. In its simplest interpretation, ritual is a series of actions performed according to a prescribed order.

Scientists and psychologists alike are taking a renewed interest in the impact ritual can have on our overstimulated, overstuffed brains. There is evidence to suggest that rituals can have an anxiolytic quality – that is, anxiety-busting effects. Psychologist Nick Hobson argues that it is the "repetitive and rigid" movements of rituals that create within us feelings of order and control around our personal environment, negating the effects of uncertainty. The brain is essentially tricked into thinking it's experiencing a pleasant state of predictability and stability.

How different might life feel if we carved out a series of rituals to return to? In our over-scheduled, chaotic lives, it might feel quaint to commit to a fish dinner on a Friday or special trips rounded off with beans on toast, but these simple pleasures might be exactly what we need.

I learned from John that in the repeated actions of ritual we can find comfort and solace. As the passage of time marches on and we see our loved ones start to change, finding an anchor in these simple, ordinary practices can help us retain a sense of the familiar as the world transforms around us.

Being unashamedly ourselves

Another charming elder I had the joy of including in a documentary was Ursula. As soon as I started chatting to her, I was struck by her curious accent: she had a distinctive German twang, masked by thick layers of Cockney.

As I settled into her armchair she told me that she was born in Hamburg and lived through the Allied bombing of her hometown during the Second World War. But war was boring and life was for living. One day, while enjoying a trip to the fairground, she met a handsome British solider. She couldn't speak English, but managed some simple conversation, persuading him to come home and meet her parents, who were far from delighted at this prospect.

133

Despite her parents' protestations, Ursula married her fairground-beau and moved to the UK. She soon learned English and acquired a penchant for Cockney rhyming slang.

Sitting and sharing these tales was a celebration for both of us. I loved Ursula. She made me chuckle with glee and proclaim: "I want to be like her when I grow up." For Ursula, it was an exercise in being noticed, again. At the age of 84, she had become invisible, rarely asked to offer her voice and experience.

She had so much to offer and we soon sat Ursula down in front of a camera to tell her life story. She was full of wicked humour and walked us through her experiences and their ups and downs as if she was waltzing through a party, entertaining the guests with a series of devilishly constructed anecdotes. She was a documentary maker's dream.

During the course of the interview, Ursula told us that she had lost her husband to lung cancer. She paused for a moment and reflected on his life: "He wasn't the greatest lover but at least I could rely on him." And those eyes of hers twinkled. This 84-year-old was so unashamedly herself, it was an absolute delight to behold.

"THE THING ABOUT BEING OLD IS IT'S SUCH A RELIEF. YOU'VE REALIZED THAT TRYING TO CHANGE WHO YOU ARE IS NO GOOD. SO YOU SETTLE INTO YOURSELF"

Many months later when we edited the footage, it felt fun and very "Ursula" to include this comment and her jokes about chasing handsome doctors around the hospital. I rang her to see whether I could pop over for a cup of tea and to show her the edited interview, to be met with the sad news that she had passed away. Her daughter told me she'd love to see the film and that, in a few weeks' time, I should come to the family home.

I spent lots of time fretting over some of Ursula's bolder comments, particularly the "lover" line. Imagine! A deceased woman commenting upon the sex life of her deceased husband. Surely it would offend her family deeply?

I held my nerve. Ursula's daughter watched her mother's interview, deeply moved by all the beautiful memories captured on film, many of which she'd never heard before. I braced myself as the line "he wasn't the greatest lover" approached, and was met with a howl of laughter from Ursula's daughter. "There couldn't be a more fitting tribute to my mother," she snorted, "leave it in."

And just like that, Ursula was immortalized as a woman who boldly lived life as a humorous adventure. I often think of her when life feels particularly heavy or tiresome. Ursula didn't need to carry the burden of life heavily, and neither must we.

SELF-ACCEPTANCE AND THE RELIEF OF BEING OLD

One January, I packed myself off to Kerala for a yoga retreat. As I arrived, jet-lagged, our teacher whispered to me: "You are, um, the youngest guest. Quite a bit younger."

I've always enjoyed being the youngest in a group so I can occupy the position of student, so I remained unfazed. That was, until I walked into the first group meeting and discovered that I had somehow accidentally booked myself onto what appeared to be a "senior" retreat. We went around the room introducing ourselves and I was shocked to discover that almost everyone was, indeed, over 60 and that the oldest guest was approaching 80. Two weeks suddenly felt like a daunting prospect.

After the initial panic and a frenzied online search for other retreats to escape to, I caught myself and decided to see what I could learn from this unconventional set of holiday companions. As the fortnight unfolded, I was humbled beyond belief. Not only were my fellow yogis far more supple and persistent than I with the difficult poses, but they had a lightness of being that I longed for. I'd arrived somewhat frazzled but by spending time with people who had the carefree perspective of age, I softened and uncoiled.

Sitting with them one evening sharing a curry, I recall Nan, the true elder of the group, saying to me: "the thing about being old is it's such a relief. You've realized that trying to change who you are is no good. So you settle into yourself." She could sense the nervous energy of my youth, trying to work out who I was, and the overwhelm that comes with the luxury of choice. I was spending a lot of time fretting about which career opportunities I should pursue and worrying that, by choosing one path, I was closing off other ones. From the vantage point of being 80, making choices didn't feel so grave. Nan kindly told me: "any of those options will work out fine and then there will be a new set of choices to face". I could feel myself relaxing, a decision about which six-month work project to take no longer feeling so terrifying. "Life is long," she reminded me, with the subtext: "chill out, young one".

The relief of old age that Nan talked of was so simple and so comforting. She had developed an uncomplicated but crucial philosophy: whatever happens, we will be OK. Each day, the sun will rise and we will face what lies ahead. We become stronger through experiencing difficult things over and over in different forms and coming out the other side. Living life is itself a celebration. But, more than that, the more we learn to celebrate, the more we are able to enjoy the journey.

Over the fortnight I realized just how precious passing wisdom between generations is. This should not be a new revelation at all, but with no living grandparents left, it dawned on me how much of my social engagement was with my peers. How so many of us seek out wisdom from those at the same life stage as us, rather than those who have lived through it. I've started to seek out more time with elders, bringing them together in a collective that I run called Sister Stories, where having women from the ages of 19 to 70 coming together to share their experiences feels a treat. With communities becoming more fragmented and isolated, it feels strange and radical to come together in this way. But this kind of communion is what we were designed for, an act as natural as sitting round a campfire.

How could our lives and communities be enriched if we all actively sought more connection across generations, where we all had dual roles as student and teacher, learning from those older than us and passing on what we know to those younger than us? And how could we help ourselves enjoy life by letting ourselves off the hook a bit more, so every decision and action didn't seem so terribly serious? In my most tense moments I think of Nan, on the yoga mat, having collapsed out of an arm balance and having a good old chuckle at herself. I was worried that at her age she was too frail to be tumbling about. She had no such worries. Just her laughter lines.

GET THE LISTENING HABIT

Ideas for enjoying life

1 | DEVELOPING RITUALS
What habits or traditions can we find to help bring a sense of stability in a changing world? Whether alone or shared, establish some joyful, simple habits.

2 | COMMUNITY AND CONNECTION
Where could you develop relationships with people of different ages? Make a commitment to broaden your social circle and see what that brings to your life.

3 | GLEAMING DETAIL
Listen with big ears and boundless curiosity to any story another being begins to share with you. Don't be afraid to ask questions, get curious and tease out the gleaming detail in the story. Remember, it can lie within the ordinary.

4 | SIMPLE CELEBRATION
Celebrating together, even when we are not feeling totally connected, can be positively powerful. Celebration rituals can be as simple as beans on toast on a Friday. How simple can you get with your ways of celebrating with others?

5 | HUMOROUS ADVENTURE
Look for any opportunity to live life lightly as a humorous adventure. Remembering the fleeting nature of our mortality is a great leveller and a reminder to see the comedy within it all!

6 | CELEBRATING THANKS
What are the things in life worth celebrating? Make a weekly list of the things you've enjoyed or are proud of and cultivate a gratitude practice – it's positively good for you.

CHAPTER 10

THINKING

TRICKS

THINKING TRICKS

Common sense for a complicated world

Ruth Williams | Department Store for the Mind

We can choose the thoughts that run through our head, create a dialogue, debate and take a little control. Sometimes it's easy to do, sometimes it helps to talk our thinking through with a trusted other being. Here are a few of my tried-and-tested "thinking tricks" that get me through the day and lead to a little more lightness in my life.

Every thinking trick requires a moment of reflection, free of further judgment. I find that breathing and checking in with myself first helps. Noticing the breath, then deepening and slowing my breathing to create a sense of space. If I'm focusing on my mind, I just notice how my body is feeling, and vice versa: if the body is overwhelming my sensations, I check on what thoughts are running through my mind. More aware, I can make choices because I understand my starting point.

Below, I draw upon a hybrid of my own learning based on a positive psychology focus and the structural breakdown of cognitive behavioural therapy (CBT). The peace, space and release from judgment offered through a mindful approach to life, I feel, runs throughout all these thinking tricks. Often there is overlap across the theories and approaches that becomes simpler and clearer when you put the thinking into action.

LET IT GO

Off to work one sunny morning, I approach the roundabout at the end of my road. The car coming toward me drives into me at the point it enters the roundabout. Everything slows, I momentarily realize what is about to

" "

WE CAN
CHOOSE THE
THOUGHTS
THAT RUN
THROUGH OUR
HEAD, CREATE
A DIALOGUE,
DEBATE AND
TAKE A LITTLE
CONTROL

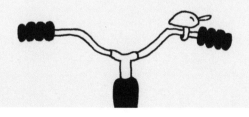

happen and reduce my speed. I notice every detail of the sound, the metallic bang on impact, followed by a slow, grinding crunch, the jolt through my body beginning at the feet and ending with a slight whiplash at the neck. I'm not hurt.

Both cars pull over. A blaze of indignant anger runs through me. I had right of way! I pause, breathe and think: "I feel angry. Focusing on who is to blame won't help. No one wanted this to happen. The most important thing is to make sure everyone is physically and emotionally safe. Let's work out the next steps together." I'm trying to recognize how I'm feeling, then letting it go, so I can move into a more logical way of weighing up the situation. I step out of the car. The other driver is still in her seat. I go over, she's in her late seventies and shaking. In the back seat is a little boy of around six or seven. Her car looks like a wreck, mine is just dented. Fortunately, no one is hurt. We work it out together. I end up taking her and the little boy to school and then staying with her until her husband arrives.

Later that day I'm hit with a wave of sadness and feel tired. I need a few moments and a hot cup of tea to recover. Even letting go and rationalizing in the moment left me with a wave of emotion, a mini post-traumatic stress experience, to address later. At this point I make space to look after myself and recover.

Learning to let go of anger allows you to create more space for accepting yourself, in several ways. While your mood is shaped by an angry response to others, you may become somewhat overwhelmed by this and have little space left to create an accepting sense of peace within yourself. When you feel anger, your mood is driven by your transactions with others, who are in some part given the control of your feelings. When you make the choice to let go of the anger you feel, then you break this control and put yourself back in the driving seat. On a deeper level, the anger we project is frequently based on a fear or anxiety about ourselves that we see reflected in the behaviour of others. If we no longer become angry about the fault we see in them, we can also set free our inner criticism of the same trait within ourselves. Abandoning anger often benefits us far more than the other person. We feel back in control and more at peace, having released some of our inner criticism.

Whatever the size of the thing you might need to let go of, these steps can still be applied:

- First, honestly recognize your emotions. At this point it is often helpful to remember that people don't make one another feel and do things, we virtually always have choices. This can help with releasing any unhelpful emotions.

- Second, look logically at the situation and gather the facts.

- Third, take action to best look after yourself emotionally and physically and, where relevant, others.

- Finally, give yourself the time that you need to recover.

SOMETIMES IT'S OK TO GET LOST

In my early twenties, while driving around Australia, my campervan companion and I decided to choose the direction we'd travel randomly when we came across a junction. We had no real time constraints and our only aim was to discover adventure and new experiences. It was fun, silly and a statement about how we were feeling at the time. It was a celebration of getting lost.

Hours and hours were spent day after day philosophizing about the world, luxuriating in existential angst, then laughing about the ridiculousness of the way we were living the stereotype.

Getting lost in the Australian desert was easy to do. We had the luxury of having assured ourselves a relative degree of safety. Our van could drive only on the bitumen roads and we had food and water on board for many days. We'd also completed a basic car-maintenance course and carried some spare parts. We had allowed ourselves to get lost only after considerable preparation for the event.

A warm sense of freedom came from knowing that no one was watching us. This was the late 1990s and, with no smartphones, far less internet use and GPS only within the grasp of the technologically savvy and wealthy, no one

really knew exactly where we were. I remember this time as the most liberating of my life. Sometimes not only is it OK to get lost, but, more often, creating occasional space for it, whether physically or metaphorically, is essential.

Over the months, while I travelled, I met others in the same wandering state. We all shared a sense of space, an openness to new things and spontaneity, a willingness to share and listen and, nearly always, at least a slight sense of anticipation. When you are lost, intentionally or not, and whether in the physical environment or on the path of life, it is usually a temporary state. Being lost felt like a cleansing of the past, a creation of space for the next chapter to be written. Sometimes we need the space to wander with nothing to do, with no social-media account to update. We just need to switch off the digital noise and let fate decide at the next junction, however small, large, brief or enduring the consequences may be. Sometimes, getting lost is really being found.

GO WITH YOUR GUT

A new baby is a scary thing. Priding myself on coping with anything life could throw at me made it harder to admit I was struggling. This new, beautiful, tiny, vulnerable being awakened within me an intense pull of diverse emotions that I had never before believed to be possible. The breastfeeding hormones rocketed the emotional volume up to a metaphorically ear-bleeding level. I reached out for books and websites and found a dizzying whirlpool of contradictory parenting advice. Everything I read seemed to be a doctrine I must follow or risk stepping into that most feared territory of being a "bad mother". The more I read and tested out on my tiny little one, the more confused I felt.

Some time passed, and I realized I was losing touch with my instincts. My head was full of advice and my body was reacting to the confusion. The stress affected my breathing a little and caused my heart to race. As I drew my baby close to feed, he felt it, too, and was restless. The wriggling created wind as he went on and off the breast. Wind led to wailing and a whole host of discomfort for all involved. Something had to give.

I stopped reading and started sensing. I got out of my head and back into my body, remembering the importance of trusting the details of what I could notice myself about what was happening, and how both baby and I felt. As judgments crept in, from the ghosts of advice and my inner critical voice, I acknowledged the sound but let the voices drift away, bringing focus back to the here and now. I noticed how my baby's breath mirrored my own: by calming myself, he became calm. I noticed how much touch helped. The closer we were, the easier it became. I used my sling in the house and started getting around more. The relief of being able to be active while nourishing my child was huge. I felt more free, lighter and had more time to just be and play.

Advice and guidance are often very helpful. However, there is something incredibly important about absorbing all these sources, then stepping back, forgetting it all and responding to your own senses and emotions. There is wisdom and confidence to be unearthed within us all.

IT AIN'T ALWAYS LIKE THAT

With the less-than-snappy label of "attribution bias", this psychological idea needs a little expansion. We all tend to think about the things that we and others do with our own version of reality in mind. This bias is not a terrible thing that we should be ashamed of, it is just something that all of us do. We only have access to the information available to us and can therefore only base our decisions on this information.

"THE TRICK IS TO QUESTION"

One way to watch out for this bias is if you take a small event and assume it always applies. Perhaps you accidentally knock a glass off the table and exclaim, "I am so clumsy! This always happens to me!" In reality, we all knock things over at times and labelling yourself clumsy is only likely to make any accidents of this sort much bigger in your mind, inaccurately reinforcing the label.

You can read a lot more in the psychological literature about the types of bias we encounter; there are nearly seven decades of theory and debate to digest, if you feel so inclined. But the pragmatic take-home from the research is that reality is almost always perception. There is no absolute fact, and so acting upon it as though there is may lead to unfavourable consequences. Many people struggle with the ambiguity this realization might bring, while others discover a sense of liberation in a lifting of the weight of absolute accuracy.

What it means for day-to-day living is that it is wise to be aware of how you make judgments. It is worth testing where the evidence comes from on which you make judgments. Approach the exercise with as much objectivity as you can muster. Retaining an openness to the potential truth of other options can be useful. This belief, or intention, can make you more approachable, less defensive, increase your connection with others and build your capacity to learn. Even more, it can increase happiness.

The trick is to question. The questions may take the form of a little inner debate with yourself or may happen through a discussion with others. Watch your language for absolutes and if you hear them creep in, take a moment to check what your conviction is based on. Aim to entertain the possibility of another way or perhaps an alternative explanation.

Earlier in this book, I told the story of an inspiring woman I interviewed about her athletic achievements (see Chapter 2, page 33, and Chapter 6, page 84). After doing my research, but before the interview, I had put her on a pedestal somewhat. I'd assumed she was a high performer with few moments of anything less than competitive success. Ten minutes into our interview I discovered that the story of her athletic achievements began later in life after experiencing postnatal depression. I was surprised, and somewhat unprepared, because of the story I'd already created in my own mind. It was a lesson for me in preparation for interviewing, and also in remembering to apply my own rhetoric by examining the easy bias I could slip into. Perhaps my questions would have been different if I'd tested my bias as part of my process.

NOT EVERYTHING WILL BE OK, BUT MOST THINGS WILL

Letting go of the weight of perfectionism can not only be a relief, but can also open your eyes to the value of a different way of approaching things. At work, the desire and drive to be perfect can be a source of stress for many of us.

In the year 2000 I worked for a consultancy that supplied assessments measuring ability and providing insights about personality using computer-based software. My role was to go to the client's workplace, install the software and hardware (a now very outdated dongle), then deliver interactive training. On each occasion the client had a different computer system with different problems, and every time there was a glitch with the projector. When I started the training, I would be awake the night before worrying about all the things that might go wrong and running repeatedly through what I would do. By the time I arrived I was decidedly wobbly inside and a wave of dread ran through me as technical problems emerged. It was exhausting and I needed a new way of thinking about this work.

Life is what happens in the spaces between planned events. The chats I had while waiting for the IT team gave me an insight into each company that I would never have discovered in the more formal training situation. When the software failed and I demonstrated how to fix it, I was also teaching the attendees how to troubleshoot without me. The most wonderful consequence of these technical issues, however, was that the atmosphere changed. The attendees' fear of failure or anxiety about asking a "silly" question (although there's no such thing in my training room) was lifted. When people relaxed into being themselves without that fear, they learned and shared so much more. A dodgy dongle provided an unexpected way to connection and fun.

The new mindset with which I approached my training delivery was to look forward to the challenge of the next technical problem. I hoped it would happen, so the mood was relaxed and the attendees were themselves. With this in mind, the night before the event became much more restful.

Re-framing your thoughts isn't just about thinking up something randomly positive. If you do that, it will feel trite and not persuasive at all. I've got to believe my own positivity, it needs to mean something to me and the things that are important to me. There's a large dose of trial and error or, for a positive re-frame, thinking about all those ups and downs in life more as an experiment. For me this means trying things out and learning from what I discover. The worry of failure drifts away, as the inner critical chatter finds peace and quiet. I rest easy in the knowledge that not everything will be OK, but most things will.

THE ANSWERS ARE EVERYWHERE –
SEEK FIRST TO UNDERSTAND

It's a weekday morning and I am facing the challenge (or experiment) of getting everyone out of the door to school and nursery. Henry's not so happy. With test practice and preparation becoming an increasing part of his day, school is rapidly losing any allure and becoming a source of anxiety. Just as we are about to leave he throws down his coat, pulls off his shoes and runs upstairs: "I'm not going! You can't make me." My first feelings are of frustration: "We will be late! I'll look like a bad mother in front of the school secretary and all the other mums and dads. He must be there on time."

"QUESTIONS AND LISTENING REALLY HELP
YOU OUT OF SO MANY TRICKY SPOTS"

Following Henry upstairs, I call out, "Come on, we'll be late, we'll have to go in through the office." Henry digs his heels in deeper. The more I push with my agenda, the more he pushes with his. Time for another way of thinking. I challenge myself:

Q: What's most important about going to school?

A: Mmmm, how about "developing a love of learning"?

This comes from one of my strengths (things about my character that are meaningful for me and bring me happiness and satisfaction; see also Chapter 4, page 64). I silence my critical parent voice, appeal to my own "love of learning" strength and seek to change my approach. The new thought running through my head is:

"Henry needs reassurance. We are not leaving until he feels confident and motivated to go to school. When he feels like that, he will be ready to learn. Being late just doesn't matter or have any serious repercussions. My job is to try to fully understand what's going on for him."

With this in mind, I go to him, sit down, give him a cuddle and just wait for Henry to take the lead and talk. He shares a few worries, we work out a plan, then think about a couple of things to look forward to at school. Eventually he decides he's ready and goes downstairs to find his coat. This took a couple of minutes and we made it to school just as his classmates were wandering in, following their usual wiggly line.

Influencing anyone to do anything anywhere or at any time in life nearly always requires an understanding of where they are, what they are thinking and what they believe to be effective. The temptation is to present, sell or push your own agenda first. Questions and listening really help you out of so many tricky spots. The answers are everywhere, we just need to know how to become curious. The place to focus first is on the thoughts kicking around in your mind. Aim to shape them so that you, too, become curious. Here are some phrases that help me:

"I want to fully understand what is going on for you."

"Your ideas and conclusions come from a place that makes complete sense for you."

"If I understand what you think and feel, I have a better chance of seeing where we connect, and where the differences lie. We can build on where we connect."

YOUR OWN THINKING TRICKS

Creating your own life manual of thinking tricks can be a creative, fun and useful exercise. You could draw upon some of the theories, reflect on what you already do that works and pick the brains of friends and family. What we have offered here is just a start of the wealth of ideas available. Perhaps you could design your own categories and chapters to act as useful reference, and to guide to any sticky points in life. These tricks can also be useful when things are going well, too. They can give you a boost, lift you higher and open your eyes to wider options.

GET THE THINKING-TRICKS HABIT

Ideas for lightness in life

1 | REVIEW NOW
Notice what works well for you in your daily life now, and also at times when you get stuck and find it hard to imagine a different approach.

2 | BREAK IT DOWN
Take one situation. Break down what happens within it. Think of each little event and the subsequent consequences as a chain of steps like the lines of a computer program. Notice which lines work and which ones lead to consequences you would rather avoid.

3 | JUST NOTICE
Notice what happens, without adding the weight of worrying about what is right or wrong. Try to remember this process is about identifying what you can control (your thoughts and behaviour) and making more conscious choices.

4 | ACCEPT
Before applying the next step, take time to notice and aim to accept where you are. Remember you do the best you can with the resources available to you.

5 | WHICH TRICK?
Draw on the thinking tricks within this chapter to test out alternatives for the steps in the computer program that lead to consequences you would like to avoid.

6 | NOTICE CHANGE
Notice what happens immediately and over time when you put the alternative into action. Aim to notice not only the practical consequences but also the emotions and sensations in your body.

EXTRAS

REFERENCES,
RESOURCES
AND CREDITS

REFERENCES
All websites accessed January 2018

Chapter 1
Kaufman, Barry Neil. (1994) *Happiness is a Choice*. New York, Ballantine Books

Seligman, Martin E P and Csikszentmihalyi, Mihaly. (2014) "Positive psychology: an introduction". *Flow and the Foundations of Positive Psychology*, 279–98. Dordrecht, Springer

Tajfel, H and Turner, J C. (2004) "The social identity theory of intergroup behavior". *Key Readings in Social Psychology*, 276–93. New York, Psychology Press

Chapter 2
Neff, Kristin. (2011) *Self-Compassion*. New York, William Morrow

Chapter 3
Garland, E L and Kelly, A. (2016) "Trauma-Informed Mindfulness-Based Stress Reduction for Female Survivors of Interpersonal Violence: Results from Stage I RCT". *Journal of Clinical Psychology*, 72(4): 311–28

www.theguardian.com/world/2017/oct/20/women-worldwide-use-hashtag-metoo-against-sexual-harassment

McCallion, Michael. (1998) *The Voice Book: For actors, public speakers and everyone who wants to make the most of their voice*. London, Faber & Faber

www.tuc.org.uk/news/nearly-two-three-young-women-have-experienced-sexual-harassment-work-tuc-survey-reveals

Neff, Kristin. (2011) *Self-Compassion*. New York, William Morrow

Chapter 4
Seligman, Martin E P and Csikszentmihalyi, Mihaly. (2014) "Positive psychology: an introduction". *Flow and the Foundations of Positive Psychology*, 279–98. Dordrecht, Springer

Chapter 5
https://news.harvard.edu/gazette/story/2010/11/wandering-mind-not-a-happy-mind/

www.huffingtonpost.com/linda-stone/just-breathe-building-the_b_85651.html

Iyengar B K S. (2015) *Light on Yoga*. London, Harper Thorsons

Chapter 7
Mayer, Emeran A et al. (2014) "Gut Microbes and the Brain: Paradigm Shift in Neuroscience". *Journal of Neuroscience*. 34(46): 15490–6

Pace, T W W et al. (2009) "Effect of Compassion Meditation on Neuroendocrine, Innate Immune and Behavioral Responses to Psychosocial Stress". *Psychoneuroendocrinology*. 34(1): 87–98

Shahar, B *et al.* (2015) "A Wait-List Randomized Controlled Trial of Loving-Kindness Meditation Programme for Self-Criticism". *Clinical Psychology & Psychotherapy.* 22(4): 346–56

theibsnetwork.org

Chapter 8
Gilbert, Elizabeth. (2016) *Big Magic: Creative Living Beyond Fear.* London, Bloomsbury

www.health.harvard.edu/staying-healthy/blue-light-has-a-dark-side

www.ted.com. www.ted.com/talks/mihaly_csikszentmihalyi_on_flow

Chapter 9
Interviews from "24 Hours in A&E" (Channel 4), courtesy of The Garden Productions

Buster, Bobette. (2013) *Do Story: How to tell your story so the world listens.* London, The Do Book Co.

Emmons, Robert. (2007) *Thanks! How the New Science of Gratitude Can Make You Happier.* Boston, Houghton Mifflin Harcourt

ww.huffingtonpost.com/randy-kamen-gredinger/the-transformative-power-_2_b_6982152.html

www.psychologytoday.com/blog/ritual-and-the-brain/201709/the-anxiety-busting-properties-ritual

Chapter 10
Covey, Stephen R. (1989) *The seven habits of highly effective people: Powerful habits in personal change.* New York, Simon & Schuster

Evans, Jonathan. (1990) *Bias in Human Reasoning: Causes and Consequences (Essays in Cognitive Psychology).* Hove, Psychology Press

Greenberger, D and Padesky, C A. (2015). *Mind Over Mood, Second Edition: Change How You Feel by Changing the Way You Think.* New York, The Guilford Press

Seligman, Martin. (2011) *Flourish: A New Understanding of Happiness and Well-Being - and how to Achieve Them.* London, Nicholas Brealey Publishing

155

RESOURCES

Websites
Try the Tara Brach Loving Kindness meditation.
www.tarabrach.com/guided-meditation-loving-kindness

More on Meredith Whitely's belly-calming tips.
www.foodatheart.co.uk

Useful ideas and guidance.
www.psychologytoday.com

Watch Martin Seligman talk about a new era of psychology.
www.ted.com/talks/martin_seligman_on_the_state_of_psychology

Discover more about positive psychology and the work of Martin Seligman.
www.authentichappiness.sas.upenn.edu

Discover and build upon your character strengths.
www.viacharacter.org

A comprehensive explanation of Kristin Neff's work and many suggestions for resources.
www.self-compassion.org

Brené Brown's website, encouraging people to be simultaneously vulnerable and brave.
www.brenebrown.com

Learn about transformational breath work and access support to develop this for yourself.
www.thebreathingroom.co.uk

Become part of the healing power of sharing and hearing stories with other women.
www.sisterstories.co.uk

Bring a gentle stretch into your life with Jackie Field.
www.mtbforfitness.com

To find support and services for people with Autistic Spectrum Disorders
In the UK: www.autism.org.uk
In the US: www.autism-society.org

Learn more about triathlons.
britishtriathlon.org

Books

Achor, Shawn. (2011) *The Happiness Advantage: The seven principles of positive psychology that fuel success and performance at work*. London, Virgin Books

Germer, Christopher K. (2009) *The Mindful Path to Self-Compassion: Freeing Yourself from Destructive Thoughts and Emotions*. New York, Guilford Press

Hamilton, David R. (2015) *I Heart Me: The Science of Self-Love*. London, Hay House

Mainemelis, C, Boyatzis, R E and Kolb, D A. (2002) "Learning styles and adaptive flexibility. Testing experiential learning theory". *Management Learning* 33(1): 5–33.

Mayer, Emeran. (2016) *The Mind-Gut Connection: How the Hidden Conversation Within Our Bodies Impacts Our Mood, Our Choices, and Our Overall Health*. New York, Harper Wave

Spector, Tim. (2016) *The Diet Myth: The Real Science Behind What We Eat*. London, Weidenfeld & Nicolson

CREDITS

Thank you to our talented authors, artists and designers who share our belief that, yes, it is more than OK to like yourself:

Ruth Williams
www.deptstoreforthemind.com
Business Psychologist and Director at Department Store for the Mind.

Aimee Hartley
www.thebreathingroom.co.uk
Talented transformational breath coach, yoga teacher, wonderful listener and great storyteller.

Meredith Whitely
www.foodatheart.co.uk
Meredith founded Food at Heart to offer people space to develop a more conscious way of eating and living.

Gemma Brady
www.sisterstories.co.uk
Documentary maker, storyteller, women's coach and the founder of the inspirational Sister Stories.

Karolin Schnoor
www.karolinschnoor.co.uk
A German freelance illustrator based in New York. With a leaning to the feminine, Karolin captures softness, joy and strength simultaneously with seeming ease.

Supafrank (Design and Creative Direction)
www.supafrank.com
A collaborative design studio, run by Katie Steel. Developing brands that speak to real human beings.

Chloe Robertson
www.chloesoffice.com
Hand-drawn patterns by Chloe Robertson.

Nicky Collings
www.nickycollings.com
Character strengths info graphic.

NOTES